*Twayne's United States Authors Series*

EDITOR OF THIS VOLUME

Warren French

*Indiana University*

*Randall Jarrell*

TUSAS 398

*Randall Jarrell*

# RANDALL JARRELL

By SISTER BERNETTA QUINN, O. S. F.
*Norfolk State University*

TWAYNE PUBLISHERS
A DIVISION OF G. K. HALL & CO., BOSTON

**Library of Congress Cataloging in Publication Data**
Quinn, Mary Bernetta.
Randall Jarrell.

(Twayne's United States authors series)
Bibliography: p.157–66
Includes index.
1.   Jarrell, Randall, 1914–1965—Criticism and
interpretation.
PS3519.A86Z75          811'.52          80-24892
ISBN 0-8057-7266-9

for Randall Jarrell

# Contents

# About the Author

Born in Lake Geneva, Wisconsin, Sister Bernetta Quinn is a member of the Franciscans of Rochester, Minnesota, in which state she taught for twenty years at the College of Saint Teresa in Winona. Author of several books, among them The Metamorphic Tradition In Modern Poetry (Rutgers University), containing the first extensive appreciation of Randall Jarrell, and Ezra Pound An Introduction to the Poetry (Columbia University Press), she frequently contributes essays and poetry to such quarterlies as The Southern Review, Contemporary Literature, and The Greensboro Review. After her 1969 participation in a Black Studies institute at North Carolina Central University in Durham, North Carolina, Sister Bernetta served on the faculty of Allen University in Columbia, South Carolina until 1972, when she moved to Norfolk, Virginia, where she is Professor of English at Norfolk State University. In 1976–1977, during a leave of absence, she conducted courses in recent American literature at Meiji Gakuin University and the University of the Sacred Heart in Tokyo.

Through sojourns at MacDowell Colony, Yaddo, the Rockefeller Villa in Bellagio, Ossabaw and elsewhere, in addition to grants from the National Foundations on the Arts and of the Humanities, she has continued to combine her work as educator with that of practitioner in criticism and poetry. Summer experiences have included teaching at the International Yeats Summer School in Sligo, the State University of New York at Buffalo, the Catholic University of America, and Siena College in Loudonville, New York, the last-mentioned of which awarded her an honorary degree. Currently, she is assembling a book of lyrics entitled Dancing in Stillness.

# Preface

It is safe to conjecture that the next decade will see a wealth of critical works on Randall Jarrell, as the last has on Flannery O'Connor, Robert Lowell, and Sylvia Plath. Hopefully, some day an entire volume can be given to Jarrell and Rilke as their geniuses intertwined. If Pound's is "a name to come," despite the plethora of books on him, Randall Jarrell's is also, although critical biographies have been slow in appearing. He himself would not regret this slowness: to him, the poetry sufficed.

In these pages, after a chapter of general introduction, a vertical approach obtains, based on the belief that dwelling on a strictly limited number of types of lyrics and subjects will be more enlightening than brief comments on a great many poems. I have tried, moreover, to extend rather than rephrase my own earlier criticism, wherein metamorphosis, symbolic landscape, key images in Jarrell are traced throughout his writing as a whole, an exception being lingering analyses of "the remembered child" as this figure informs the last collection.

Here such analyses are accorded "Lady Bates" and "A Girl in a Library," dramatic monologues once removed, since neither is heard by its addressee. Both are typical of the identification, often through the opposite sex, that enables Jarrell to disclose understandings about lives and Life. "Burning the Letters" and "Eighth Air Force," plumbed in like manner, are representative of the war poems which have won for a theorist of air battles the title of best spokesman for World War II. Uncongenial as was that phase of our century to Jarrell's sensibility, no choice but to focus on it was possible for one who felt that the poet's duty was to trade the sufferings of others for his own.

The longest chapter explores again through detailed explication of a handful of poems, Jarrell's way of making new through related arts the painting and sculpture he loved. His special "visions and revisions" are not only interesting to the expert in the university but, were they incorporated into a Humanities course, would be a splendid way to introduce young readers to him, if they are not already friends through his children's classics.

The three of these classics uniquely appreciated and "decorated" by fellow-artist Maurice Sendak—*The Bat-Poet, The Animal Family*, and *Fly by Night*—are taken as a single story of autobiographical import in Chapter 5, one united by the motif of "search-for-a-mother," put in terms as timeless as the fairy-tale beginning. The Sendak trilogy, as reviewers have recognized, displays how a very unusual human being felt about his art, and the life art imitates.

Jarrell's prose for adults—the single novel *Pictures from an Institution* (composed to repeated playings of Schöenberg's *Transfigured Night*); the translations perhaps better referred to as adaptations in that they were not derived from original texts; and the criticism which "turned about" the course of that genre in his age—is gathered together in the sixth chapter. Like the poems and children's books, it is a form of autobiography, soon to be enriched by the definitive collection of letters in preparation by Mary von Schrader Jarrell. Through the criticism he was a teacher far beyond his salaried role as such, a determiner of taste qualified by a talent for humor and an instinct for the great over the good.

Though the glass of memory is never true, each reflection being in the eye of the beholder, the concluding chapter looks into it in order to glimpse vicariously those years in Greensboro when his critical and poetic genius was at its height.

In acknowledging obligations, I owe my first acquaintance with Randall Jarrell to Frederick J. Hoffman (d. 1968) for his energetic and independent interpretation of the poet in lectures at the University of Wisconsin in Madison; without the stimulus of investigating metamorphosis under his "non-directive direction," I might not have had the benefit of Jarrell's responses to my initial criticism of him, both before and after its appearance in *The Metamorphic Tradition in Modern Poetry*, over a quarter of a century ago. His letters to me, from 1949 to 1960, are now at the Berg Collection of the New York Public Library.

The most consistent source of light in my scholarship on Jarrell has been Mary von Schrader Jarrell, whose devoted and intelligent interest has been of help to so many motivated by a wish to increase Randall's audience, who have always numbered many more than the few he considers them in "A Conversation with the Devil." Without her diligent editing and commenting, the work on Jarrell would have remained fragmentary; I join all his other critics in saying a simple "Thanks."

A book such as this, even when duplication of its author's work is avoided, leans upon what came before on its subject; credit for assistance having already been given, I would merely like to mention again the now-retired Donald C. Gallup, Curator of the American Literature Collection at the Beinecke Rare Book and Manuscript Library at Yale University, and his wonderfully serviceable staff; Karl Gay, director of the Lockwood Memorial Poetry Library of the State University of New York in Buffalo; Sue Davis of Queen's College in Charlotte, North Carolina; Lola Sladitz, Curator of the Berg Collection at the New York Public Library; Sister Eone Kling, O.S.F., and Sister Tressa Piper, O.S.F. of the College of Saint Teresa Library in Winona, Minnesota, together with the various library staffs in Norfolk, Virginia, where John Parker of Kirn Memorial was particularly helpful, and at the University of Wisconsin in Madison

While teaching at the University of the Sacred Heart and Meiji Gakuin University in Tokyo, 1976–77, I received welcome bibliographical materials from Suzanne Ferguson, as well as even more welcome encouragement, then and later. Japan also offered a chance to exchange insights with Fumihisa Matsumoto, probably the first scholar in that country to do a master's thesis on Randall Jarrell (Keio University), who visited me weekly for conferences on his Jarrell translations, over fifty of which he expects to publish soon in Tokyo; he is currently pursuing a doctorate in American Studies on a National Endowment grant at Yale University. During the year in Japan, Professor Toshikazu Niikura of the Meiji Gakuin English faculty advanced my project not only through his fine departmental library and congenial staff but also through the impetus given my research by the invitation to lecture on Jarrell at Meiji Gakuin University in June 1977.

The sharing of members of the Breyer family and of Mrs. Albert Ganier (the poet's cousin), as well as others, during a March 1979, trip to Nashville (and later) is much appreciated, as are the counsel and knowledge on that occasion proffered me by Dr. Thomas Daniel Young and the late Dr. Edgar Duncan of Vanderbilt. I am especially mindful of the kindness through correspondence of Emily Herring Wilson, Heather Ross Miller, Sylvia Wilkinson, Pat Borden, Barbara Lovell, Bertha Harris Wyland, and other former Jarrell students, who recorded for me their irreplaceable (and impermanent unless printed) memories of Jarrell. For the Prologue, first sent me by Robert Watson in a different version, I am grateful to the one-time Randall Jarrell Scholar Jim Clark. Reading again these lines that are somehow sad as youth is sad, and thoroughly romantic, as Randall was, brings home how they are speech that cats and dogs can understand, while at the same time more implicit than overt. In the letter accompanying this anniversary lyric, Clark writes: "I would like to find some way to work the bat-poet in"; as Jarrell himself did in the vulture-as-Death symbol of "The Woman at the Washington Zoo," Clark "built better than he knew," introducing the small furred winged creature without naming it, by analogy with the leaf and the quilt piece, a minor success due to his being able to count on the richly peopled landscape of memory existing in everyone who has ever been a "student" of the Bat-Poet.

Writing a book worthy of Randall Jarrell has been a goal moving always ahead, like going to Moscow in *The Three Sisters*. "Some things can be done as well as others," says Sam Patch in *Paterson* before he jumps into the Genesee River. Some things are harder than others. May readers exercise that empathy whereby the subject of this study was so adept at entering into the lives of others; may they see the difficulties, and absolve. All this book desires to do is to play a humble part in a better one.

SISTER BERNETTA QUINN, O.S.F.

*Norfolk State University*

# Chronology

1914  Born May 6, Randall Jackson Jarrell, the same birthday as Sigmund Freud, in Nashville, Tennessee, first child of Anna Campbell Jarrell and Owen Jarrell.

1922  Posed for the Ganymede of Nashville's Centennial Park Parthenon.

1926  After separation of his parents lived in Hollywood with great-grandmother and grandparents, the "Dandeen," "Mama," and "Pop" of *The Lost World*.

1931  Graduation from Hume-Fogg High School, Nashville.

1932  Sent to Vanderbilt University through the generosity of his uncle, Howell Campbell. Here he was taught by John Crowe Ransom, who considered him the best by far of the young writers in his workshop. Composed lyrics in the manner of the Fugitives. Edited the humor magazine, *The Vanderbilt Masquerader*.

1934  First published poem, "Above the waters in their toil," *American Review*.

1935  Received an A.B. from Vanderbilt and continued there as a graduate student in English, working on A. E. Housman.

1936  Met Peter Taylor, beginning a friendship of inestimable value to both.

1937  Instructor at Kenyon College in Gambier, Ohio, where he continued his Vanderbilt dissertation, Donald Davidson having replaced Ransom as mentor. At first roomed with Robert Lowell in Ransom's home. Received M. A. degree from Vanderbilt in 1938, after completion of "Implicit Generalization in Housman."

1939

1939  Taught English at the University of Texas, Austin. Married one of his colleagues, Mackie Langham, on June 1, 1939. Twenty poems appeared in John Ciardi's *Five Young American Poets* (1940). *Blood for a Stranger*, first volume of verse, brought out by Harcourt, Brace in 1942 and dedicated to Allen Tate.

1942

1942  Enlisted in the United States Army, first as pilot-trainee but after "washing out" became instructor of aviators near Tucson, Arizona, the last period of service being in Celestial Navigation classes. *Little Friend, Little Friend* published in 1945.

1946

1946  First Guggenheim Fellowship. Taught at Sarah Lawrence Col-
1947  lege, Bronxville, N.Y. Literary editor of *The Nation*. In fall,
      1947, became Associate Professor at Women's College, Univer-
      sity of North Carolina at Greensboro, with his wife, Mackie,
      also on English staff.
1948  First trip to Europe for the summer Salzburg Seminar in Amer-
      ican Civilization. *Losses* published.
1951  *The Seven-League Crutches*. Summer Writers' Conference in
      Boulder, Colorado. Visiting Professor in Literary Criticism at
      Princeton University, 1951–52. Separation from Mackie in
      September.
1952  Divorced from Mackie October 31. Married November 8 to
      Mary Eloise von Schrader. Began translating Chekhov's *The
      Three Sisters*. Taught that summer at Indiana School of Letters.
1953  *Poetry and the Age*. Taught the winter semester at the Uni-
      versity of Illinois in Urbana.
1954  *Pictures from an Institution*, his only novel. Bollingen Award
      judge.
1955  *Selected Poems*. National Book Award judge.
1956  Consultantship in Poetry at Library of Congress. Summer of
1958  1958 with Mary in Italy, near the Peter Taylors and the Robert
      Fitzgeralds. Six weeks as Guest Professor at the University of
      Cincinnati followed by appointment as full Professor in Sep-
      tember at U. of North Carolina, Greensboro.
1960  *The Woman at the Washington Zoo* wins National Book
      Award. Summer in Italy with the Peter Taylors.
1961  Edited *The Best Short Stories of Rudyard Kipling*. Read at the
      second Johns Hopkins Poetry Festival. Chapel Hill celebration
      in his honor.
1962  Translations of Bechstein and Grimm. *A Sad Heart at the
      Supermarket*. Honorary Degree from Bard College, Annan-
      dale-on-Hudson. "Fifty Years of American Poetry" lecture at
      the National Poetry Festival.
1963  Second Guggenheim. Five months in Europe, working day and
      night on *Faust* translation. Edited two more Kipling antholo-
      gies, with introductions, also *Six Russian Short Novels*.
1964  First two children's books, *The Gingerbread Rabbit* and *The
      Bat-Poet*. June 22, his *The Three Sisters* production in New
      York City. On October 29 read his and Elizabeth Bishop's
      poems, introduced by Robert Lowell, at New York City's Gug-
      genheim Museum.

1965   *The Animal Family*. Hospitalized in Chapel Hill February to late May with a breakdown. On a trip back for a skin graft, after resuming teaching, fatally hit by a car October 14 and buried October 17 in the Guilford Cemetery in Greensboro. *The Lost World* published later that year, with an appreciation by his old friend Robert Lowell.

# *Prologue*

"A Letter: After All This Time"

*for Randall Jarrell
d. 10.14.65*

I

It is mid-October, and the blood of trees
boils and burns.
knits the low-lying air in pieces
laying them down, all patchwork and brilliance.

*They are only leaves.*

*As are we, each
only a leaf.
What brilliance is ours
is ours because we do not care.*

What brilliance?
If only, after we have burned and danced and spun,
poised, just so, on the eve of our letting go—
if only we did not care.

II

That, I know, is no way to begin
whatever it is I have to say to you,
dead these dozen years. You for whose name
I journeyed, in Limbo, from Nashville
to here.

From Nashville, then, where your name
was dust on a library shelf, and old tongues
rattled on, trying to translate for me
that dust into something vibrant and quick—
a well to drink from—
but could not.

I headed east toward water,
that dust in my mouth.

### III

October the fourteenth,
and I was all afternoon fining
a poem, stalled since May.
I went to the window
and stood there awhile, looking down at the streets
still glistening from early rain.
"Strange," I thought: "Nothing moving,
and almost five o'clock." And suddenly
I remembered how you had called this place
a Sleeping Beauty, as of course you would;
and still more suddenly, recalled the final words
from *Hohensalzburg,* that clicked like a key
in the lock of what I had written:
> *We also are forever one:*
> *A dweller of the Earth, invisible.*

And that was when, from the calendar tacked to the door,
the black fourteen dropped into the final slot
of the puzzle I was trying to remember.
I went to the window and looked out again—.
Up and down the streets as far as I could see
the traffic that always was, was not there:
and I thought maybe I heard laughter
on the wind, and a voice singing:
*But where is it, where is it? O it's not there . . .*

### IV

And so it is night. The library
glows now, where an hour ago the sun
sank into trees the color of sun.

Out of the past, the dust
that was Nashville, I have come here:
this night, this courtyard, to listen
to something that dances and spins
in the trees above me; to feel

*Prologue*

cool on my forehead and face the prickle
of raindrops, knocked from leaves where they shiver;
to look up and see shining
some small light, a leaf
burning in the low-lying air—
a piece of the quilt,
all patchwork and brilliance:
                              *Only look.*
                              *I am here behind the moonlight.*

Jim Clark
*Greensboro*
10.14.77

CHAPTER 1

# An Introduction to Randall Jarrell

THOUGH all lives are necessarily linear, that of Randall Jarrell has about it a spatial form which lends itself to an analogy with landscape.[1] In childhood and adolescence he moved back and forth between Tennessee and California, during World War II from Illinois to Arizona and Texas, and later from campus to campus lecturing or reading at over a hundred, even from continent to continent. His adult career, though popular impression relates it only to Greensboro, North Carolina, resembles the progress of the wandering minstrels of Provençe and Tuscany in the late Middle Ages. Before each troubadour's poetry in libraries such as Milan's one finds a *vida* so alive with fascinating dramatic details as collectively to draw the young Ezra Pound from town to town in southern Europe, and many another in his wake. Jarrell's published life is almost as small a map of his pilgrimage as that of a medieval song-maker.

From the start, he showed himself impatient with autobiography, feeling it inappropriate as an appendage to writing which ought to stand on its own worth.[2] One of the most widely used reference books, *Twentieth-Century Authors* edited by Stanley Kunitz,[3] does not even mention Jarrell's first marriage, to Mackie Langham, though it lasted for twelve years. Surprisingly, he is included in none of the volumes of *Current Biography*. No doubt he ignored questionnaires requesting data: whatever information appears is simply repeated from book to book. Yet unavoidably, if unobtrusively, he like T. S. Eliot put himself into what he wrote, which will gradually come to be seen as his true portrait, though not for those meant by the adage "He who runs may read." Enriching this portrait eventually will be the *Letters* presently being edited by his literary executor, Mary Jarrell.[4]

## I  Childhood

Born May 6, 1914, in Nashville, Tennessee, Randall Jackson Jarrell was the son of Owen J. and Anna Campbell Jarrell, who later had a

21

second child, Charles. The insecurities he encountered during his ear-
liest and formative years can be guessed at from the city directory,
which gives frequent changes of address and sometimes only the
mother's name,[5] once with the euphemism "widow" though Owen was
alive until the 1970s. The insecurities reveal themselves as one studies
the photographs in the memorial volume put together by Robert Lowell, Peter Taylor, and Robert Penn Warren,[6] beginning with Randall
at two and a half, a sunny, chubby youngster with short blonde hair,
and followed by a snapshot taken at eight that catches a sadness, almost
a bewilderment. It was at the time of the second picture that Randall
had his first contact with the arts, serving as sculptor Belle Kinney's
model for Ganymede in the bas-relief of the west pediment in the Parthenon of Nashville's Centennial Park, near Vanderbilt University (the
only exact replica of the ancient Greek building in existence). Sitting
face full front, with legs draped over a reclining female figure, Randall
holds a horn of ambrosia against his right thigh. With his scrawny
body, he makes a rather non-Greek cupbearer of the gods, a character
presaging his being snatched up to Olympus by the divine force which
dominated the best years of his art.

Though Randall and brother Charles seem to have had little contact
after their youth, the *Southern Review* correspondence now at the
Beinecke Rare Book and Manuscript Library at Yale contains glimpses
of their relationship during the 1930s, when Charles was on the Baton
Rouge campus of Louisiana State University, where Robert Penn Warren, Cleanth Brooks, and other famous literary figures were engaged
in teaching and founding the magazine. The surrealistic "A Little
Poem" conveys something of the brothers' incompatibility ("I said, 'O
speak!' My brother smiled,/ And I saw Nothing beckon from his lids
. . ."). Had the poet been part of a large and happy family, his loneliness as a child, continuing throughout life in the depths if not on the
surface, might not have informed the poetry as it does: however, as a
subtitle in *Selected Poems* says, "The world is everything that is the
case." It was natural that Randall should have sought escape through
the exercise on his environment of his gifted sensibility: "One way of
fighting loneliness, en route to death, is through the imagination, as
many an only child has discovered, together with those children who
because of special endowments or the lack of them, certain fears or
animosities or prejudices, have found themselves isolated from other
children within the family or the neighborhood."[7]

Among the kin on his mother's side, Randall had a good rapport with his Aunt Mamie's daughter Mary, whom he renamed Bitsy;[8] "Mamie's Itsy-Bitsy," he used to call her, the designation Bitsy she kept even to the signing of checks. Five years younger than Randall, she remembers the day he took her to Centennial Park to see the stone lions, reassuring her: "They're not *real* lions—you can sit on them!" He drew for her wonderful airplanes in bright colors: "These planes will never get off the ground," he told her, "they're so thick with paint." If the boy Randall was self-absorbed, he was also sensitive to the emotions of others, as when he would try to assuage Bitsy's fear of flying by telling her that people once had been afraid of automobiles and before that of horses, a foreshadowing of the child-comforting in the mature lyrics for which he is famous. Though he did his best to teach Bitsy tennis, she proved an awkward pupil.[9] One of her favorite anecdotes concerns the night when Randall, who even then hated parties, was bundled into a tuxedo and shipped off to a dance to prevent his cousin's getting stuck without a partner. Halfway through the evening, he telephoned home to ask if he might leave, since Bitsy had most of the stag line waiting for her.

Lucie Breyer Kay remains an excellent source for "oral history" in that she went through junior high school to a Vanderbilt University degree with Randall, of whom she became aware when they were young children. He caught up with her after entering Vanderbilt a year later than she, so that they were received into the Junior Phi Beta Kappa together.[10] "The Elementary Scene" published in the *Southern Review* when he was twenty-one, is probably a collage of impressions of the school he attended previous to Tarbox Junior High, now a home for senior citizens. The poem unites the melancholy images of weeds, grass ("Trodden on, straggling, yellow and rotten," "the gaunt field," and "dead land"), a setting as dismal in retrospect as the dusty, stored emblems of Halloween which the third stanza describes in detail. Inside the building, if there were cheerful aspects Jarrell when uprooted forgot them; though "Moving" has a small girl as *persona*, it might be himself speaking: "I shall never again sing/ Good Morning, Dear Teacher, to my own dear teacher." Perhaps more typical of the school is "the Study Hour,/ Spent at a desk, with folded hands, in waiting" ("Aging"). Many of the child lyrics in *Selected Poems* are undoubtedly facets of his own experience, metamorphosed: "The Night before the Night before Christmas," "The Child of Courts," "The Black Swan," "A Sick Child," "A Quilt Pattern," the group based on borrowings from the Carnegie Library, but most of all "90 North."

This poem has been so often and so adequately annotated[11] that one hesitates to speak of it further. The little boy that it uses as focus of narration (and he must have been little to wear a flannel nightgown, to clamber up to bed) has fantasized the story of the heroic Admiral Byrd until it is his own, as elsewhere the abandoned Hansel's is. The "sufficient kingdom of the child" ("The Northern Snows") is a bed transformed in dream to a floe of ice on a curving surface, the "impossible" side of the globe, a refuge from the icy waters of the school day. The imaginer has reached the ultimate, standing at the North Pole, black-bearded, hungry, wearing furs stiff with ice, surrounded by huskies and the corpses of his frozen companions, planting the American flag in a snapping wind that contrasts with the stasis of polar ice. There is no place else to go but back to the south of his humdrum classroom, his "unbelieving" family and friends, this time hurting from the realization that none of us gets out of this world alive. The top of the earth is also the bottom.

Formerly, when the child lay cozy in his bed after a night of dreamtravels, his Protestant faith in a heavenly reward had sustained him, but now neither that light nor the "ignorant darkness" (opposites presented as the same, a device which grew more and more characteristic of Jarrell), is an answer. *Darkness* occurs six times in the last six lines. The lonely child sees that what for Byrd was victory (a challenge met) for him is defeat: darkness = pain = meaninglessness = wretchedness = darkness.

When toward the end he reconstructs that part of his youth spent out West, in "Thinking of the Lost World," his meeting with *nothing* in "90 North" has been assimilated into a kind of peace: "I hold in my own hands, in happiness,/ Nothing: the nothing for which there's no reward." "90 North" gives only the pain. Those selections that Jarrell chose to translate from Rainer Maria Rilke are also revelatory of how much weariness the sensitive boy suffered during grade school, poems like "Childhood," which begins "The time of school drags by with waiting/ And dread, with nothing but dreary things"; the mood is Rilke's, of course, and no more than "a piece" of Randall's psyche at that age. The Bitsy anecdotes prove that there was sunshine as well as desert, also the Sunday afternoon pleasure drive of "Aging," when time stood still.

The final volume, *The Lost World*, sketches in the California period to be supplemented by his accounts of it as sent to his mother in Tennessee, letters warm with filial love, though the tie was to weaken with the years. During the 1920s, Owen and Anna separated, he going out West as a photographer in the Richard Seeley Studio with branches in three Californian cities while Anna remained in Nashville. Randall went to live with "Mom and Pop" in Long Beach.[12] Since they were really his grandparents, the titles belonged to a "Let's Pretend" game comparable to that he later was to employ as a literary device. Also a member of the Long Beach family circle was "Dandeen," his great-grandmother. Life in the film capital, Hollywood, was exciting despite the uprootedness suggested in "The Prince": "After the door shuts, and the footsteps die,/ I call out, 'Mother?' No one answers" (originally entitled "The Child of Courts," an expression of his reaction to the divorce proceedings).

In the childless surroundings the boy had as company Reddy Rabbit, perhaps the prototype of the hero of *The Gingerbread Rabbit* and the dog named Reddy in *Fly by Night*, two of his children's books. The rabbit in "The Lost World" becomes a symbol of initiation into the problem of evil, where the terrifying sight of his grandmother wringing off a chicken's neck creates in the small watcher a fear that such a fate may one day overtake his pet, and by extension himself and his dear ones. This discovery of what death is through the killing of the fowl corresponds to that in John Crowe Ransom's "Janet Waking," where the little girl comes upon her chicken dead through the sting of a "transmogrifying bee." The panic it generated in Jarrell never completely left him, a panic referred to in an elegy on him by his good friend John Berryman, "Op. posth. no. 13."

In the spring of 1926 Randall reluctantly left for the East, rejected as he believed by the substitute parents, a feeling incarnated in "A Story." Returning to Tennessee meant leaving behind his Aunt Bettie ("The Lost World"), as well as the glamor of stage sets and streets as romantically named as Sunset Boulevard.[13]

Where he should have been able to find strength—in Anna, his mother—apparently he did not, any more than did Hart Crane in his unstable mother, Grace. The fainting spells of that time, so upsetting to her sons, are recorded in the late poetry, as is the absence of any real understanding in that 1940 or earlier tissue of memories "The Bad Music." Married at sixteen, and left to cope with raising Randall and Charles as a single parent, as a temporary solution Anna (Campbell) Jarrell sent the boys out to stay on Aunt Mamie's farm, where they stirred up a furor amidst the hens' eggs and beehives. This chapter of Randall's youth is no doubt the origin of the unpublished fragment

"My aunt kept turnips in a flock—/ Did you ever hear of such strange stock?" The older brother was always rescuing the younger. Somewhat inexplicably, Charles was to give his daughter the name Randall. When the boys went to visit their Uncle Pandy's luxurious home, Randall would lose himself for hours in the library while Howell, Jr., and Charles got into mischief outside.[14]

Not until "The Player Piano," and then only through a woman persona could the sensitive Randall forgive his parents for his childhood; there he writes "I don't blame you,/ You weren't old enough to know any better;/ If I could I'd go back, sit down by you both,/ And sign our true armistice: you weren't to blame."

## II  *Jarrell the Adolescent*

Jarrell's secondary-school education was at Nashville's Hume-Fogg High School, at Eighth and Broadway, a few blocks from the original Grand Old Opry House of the country music movement dating from the WMS Barn Dances, which began when he was eleven. To the city today, Dinah Shore, '34, is its most famous graduate. Randall was never one of the crowd: exclamations like "Peachie keen!" did not endear him to his masculine peers, and he was teased about his "sneakers."[15] The commencement issue of the school magazine *Echoes* labels him "Hopefully hopeless" in its "Appearance" category; "in the clouds and below" under "Always Seen"; and "To Be Appreciated" under "Greatest Ambition." The Carnegie Library was nearby, to supply the books that were his chief pleasure. When at Yale for the Gray lecture in April 1964, he told an interviewer, Steven Schatzow, how he used to read *The Waste-Land* as he rode home from high school on a bus, "only days after it was written."[16]

That so many of his lyrics are monologues with addressees is in a way foreshadowed by his interest in the Hume-Fogg Dramatic Club, which voted him into the office of Promoter during his senior year. With its members he went to see *Liliom* in November 1929. His penetrating if patronizing critique of the performance came out in *Echoes* (March 1925), this sentence revealing a sensitivity to symbols: "In Liliom we see not just a sideshow barker, but the whole race of wanderers, misunderstanding and misunderstood" (p. 17). Preston N. Bissinger, then editor of *Echoes*, recalls him as a nonconformist: "The stories he wrote for the Echo [sic] were quaint and reflected a sense of humor I was actually unable to appreciate at the time, although I accepted several of them for publication."[17] An example is "The Thanksgiving Miracle," about two Marseilles sailors marooned on a desert island, much to their boredom: "If they had been men of culture, they might have drawn in the sand with a stick, looked at themselves in the ocean, or recited poetry, but they were simple men."[18] This gentle mockery is quite exceptional for a high school underclassman.

Randall Jarrell's "Shakespeare versus Ibsen" shows flickers of the witty balances characteristic of his later essays: "Shakespeare's plays succeed only by good acting—Ibsen's plays succeed in spite of bad acting.// The reason is that Shakespeare's plays were written primarily for the actor—Ibsen's for something else" (p. 16).[19] Typical of his enthusiasms is this piece of dramatic criticism of *The Wild Duck*, the first reading of which he describes as "one of the intellectual experiences of one's life." Sometimes he left his articles unsigned, a practice kept up at Vanderbilt, but that on *Candida* could be by no one else. Even after he was graduated, he contributed to the magazine, as when José Iturbi came to Nashville in April 1932; in reviewing the concert Jarrell mentions his own piano-playing: he writes that for six months after hearing Claude Achille in a concert he played Debussy's *L'Après-Midi* each night before retiring.

Besides covering plays (for instance, a local production of *Hamlet*, a play he had practically memorized),[20] Jarrell also acted, notably in *Arms and the Man*, an ironic title in view of his noncombatant status in World War II.[21] He is also credited in the Commencement, 1931, issue of *Echoes* with membership in his senior year in the French, Debate, and Literary Clubs, while earlier, as group pictures show, he had belonged to the Music Club. In the page devoted to class officers, there is something poignant about the word *prophet* curved over Jarrell's oval profile (somber expression, one wayward lock): The Class Prophecy itself, in the same number, uses as framework two children and a Hermit (comparable to Alvin and his grandfather in *A Sad Heart at the Supermarket*); though the spoof on tradition is unintelligible to outsiders, it furnishes good sources for biographical interviews.[22]

Randall's classmate Lucie Breyer has already been mentioned. Her brother Bernard, nicknamed Budgie, five years younger, in 1947 married Randall's cousin on the maternal side.[23] But the closest to Jarrell among the Breyers was the dark-blonde, beautiful Amy, two years older than he. The Breyer mansion, then standing alone in its section of Nashville, is now a treasure-house of paintings (including originals

by Picasso and Larry Rivers). The original home was presided over by
a great lady, much admired by Jarrell. He came first as Lucie's caller
but was turned over by her to the younger sister.[24] When he needed
stimulating companionship, he could find it at the eccentric, delightful
Breyers, who seemed like people in a movie. His association with the
parents and their seven children bridged educationally the distance
between high school and university life.

### III   The Vanderbilt Days

After high school, Randall took a year out before the university,
though he continued to study in depth, concentrating on *Principia
Mathematica*, an abstruse book by Bertrand Russell and Alfred North
Whitehead with a thesis that mathematics is reducible to logic, which
a mathematician-friend assured Lucie Breyer that Randall not only
read but understood its point. While at Hume-Fogg, he had listed
under "Books that have influenced and helped me" Russell's *Philosophy*.[25] Russell's electrifying proposition that philosophy, like mathematics, confines itself to the possible whereas science confines itself to
the real gave a scope to Jarrell's thought-processes comparable to one
of those evolutionary "leaps" called by Bernard Lonergan *insight*. The
efforts of his mother's brother, Howell Campbell ("Uncle Pandy"), a
prosperous candy manufacturer, to interest him in a business career
were a failure.

Robert ("Red") Penn Warren, who taught the sophomore literature
course that Jarrell took as a Vanderbilt freshman, remembers Amy as
"a brilliant, good-looking, and charming girl, then a medical student
who was also doing a lot of graduate work in French. She and my first
wife were close friends [they had shared a Vanderbilt seminar] and she
was often at our little white-washed home in the country: I remember
that Amy sometimes darned my socks, out of the goodness of her heart,
meanwhile talking about Baudelaire. Sometimes Randall came
along."[26] Through Warren's Italian-born wife, the Warrens came to be
frequent visitors at the Breyer home, for "jolly Jewish dinners, full of
intellect and jokes. Randall was present on such occasions." The Ken-
tucky poet liked the brothers and sisters but even more the father and
mother.

By the time Amy went to New York on a prestigious internship in
pediatrics, Randall's romance with her was over, even if not to be forgotten for their lifetimes. She felt herself unequal to becoming the wife

of the prodigiously gifted person she recognized him to be. Amy married twice, between the marriages writing her old suitor who was then in the Air Force for consolation and receiving it.[27] She died a suicide in Texas in 1960, still subscribing to the literary journals that had published his work. When he last visited Vanderbilt, in 1965, he stopped into the Mills Book Store and, taking Amy's cousin, Mrs. Bernard Scheid, wife of the manager, into a back room, read her some poems he had written to Amy, poems which her Nashville sister, Lucie, and Rose Martin, keep, along with a generous sheaf of Randall's letters to Amy.[28] "When I Was Home Last Christmas," with its context of tea in a family parlor, could have been about Amy were it not for its early date and indeed may well be, even so:

> Your dead face still
> Cast me, with parted lips,
> Its tight-rope-walker's look . . . .
> But who is there now to notice
> If I look or do not look
>
> At a photograph at your mother's?
> There is no one left to care
> For all we said, and did, and thought—
> The world we were.[29]

There are different ways of being dead.

Meanwhile, Anna Jarrell was struggling to meet her financial responsibilities, teaching in an adult education program at the Watkins Institute, still at 1700 Hayes, near Hume-Fogg High School. Divorced from Owen, she had married Eugene Regan. Her ex-husband also chose another partner, further estranging himself. The rich Howell Campbell told Regan that he never made a marriage present twice to the same person; that rather than give one to Gene he would take over Randall's education (his own son, Howell, Jr.,preferred a business career to the university). Regan was killed in an automobile accident in 1940, leaving Anna once more alone.

Vanderbilt University, conservative and monied, had been founded in the 1870s through the generosity of Commodore Cornelius Vanderbilt. Jarrell's ghost returning would still be able to recognize Old Central, rechristened College Hall; the Science Hall; and Furman Hall, which now houses the humanities instead of chemistry. What in his

day was the Old Gymnasium has become a Fine Arts Center, reno-
vated. A new student union has replaced that outside of which Randall
held court in fine weather for collegians who preferred his dicta over
those of George Marion O'Donnell, leader of a rival clique. Were the
ghost to ask students lounging outside the union or in its bookstore
about his poetry, the response would very likely be "Randall Jarrell?
Who's he?" But then, as he remarked at the National Poetry Festival
in Washington in 1964 during his consultantship at the Library of Congress, the invisibility of poets in the twentieth century is general.[30]

Already a superior student in his sophomore year, he took creative
writing from John Crowe Ransom, who was to recall him as the most
talented in the class, vociferous if crossed in critical opinion. (Jarrell
would, however, mellow into a patient, considerate teacher during the
Greensboro years until he too would deserve the phrase Ransom
applied to himself on the celebration of his sixtieth birthday, "a gentleman among gentlemen" in the classroom.) Published almost as soon as
written, though not on campus, Jarrell's Vanderbilt poems were neo-
classical efforts. A representative lyric, written in 1934 but not appearing until the Collected Poems, is "O weary mariners, here shaded,
fed."

The agrarian organ The Fugitive was already history, but some of
its founding fathers were his daily associates, not that he ever "took his
stand" with them: regionalism militated against his concept of poetry.
Other friends at the University included Francis Robinson, the late
assistant manager of the Metropolitan Opera Company; Walter Sulli-
van, now on Vanderbilt's faculty in contemporary literature; Jerome
K. Small; and Seymour Samuels, a Nashville attorney. Jarrell became
editor of the Vanderbilt humor magazine, the Masquerader, providing
for its cover a drawing of the University's glamorous Sylvia Frank. As
his major he had chosen psychology, graduating with a Bachelor of
Arts degree in 1935.[31] No one, however, was surprised when the author
of "And did she dwell in innocence and joy," a Wordsworthian ode
written in 1935 (the July Southern Review), turned to the English
major for his master's degree and began work under the direction of
John Crowe Ransom. When Ransom departed for Kenyon, Donald
Davidson became Jarrell's adviser.

Ransom's confidence in his super-intelligent, lively protegé was
shown in the initial issue of The Kenyon Review, under his editorship,
when that magazine ran Jarrell's "The Winter's Tale," a poem of three
pages, and in addition "Texts from Housman," a distillation (or at least

an offshoot) of the eventually completed dissertation, "Implicit Generalization in Housman." The style of the *Kenyon Review* cutting was easy to read, not over-technical. It was excellent in its analyses of "Crossing alone the nighted ferry" and "It nods and curtseys and recovers," commentaries which Davidson himself used for many years in his Vanderbilt teaching of advanced writing courses. Ransom's confidence in the young poet and critic was shown again in the following year, 1936, when he became afflicted with an eye injury in the spring and requested Randall to take over his creative writing class; this at the time included both Peter Taylor and Bernard R. Breyer.

Davidson had had Jarrell in his English lyric class: "He was brilliant always—held his head pretty high too—could have taught the class, no doubt," he wrote Suzanne Ferguson from Bread Loaf, July 24, 1967.[32] While they got along all right, Davidson found Jarrell a bit aggressive as a student, and later, when he would come back from Kenyon for conferences on the Housman (completed in 1939), somewhat difficult to counsel, since Jarrell resisted suggestions which he felt would lessen the independence of his thinking. Davidson did manage to persuade him to insert a section on Shelley so as to meet the expectations of chairman Walter Clyde Curry, who required something "academic," fearing the project would turn out to be criticism and not scholarship. In the letter quoted from above, Davidson reveals an admiration for but hardly an affinity with this writer caught between generations: "His poetry is strange to me."

Though Randall was already in graduate school when Peter Taylor arrived from Memphis as a freshman in 1936, their compatibility was such that it initiated a long and mutually rewarding friendship, the bond deepening after Taylor's marriage in 1943 to Eleanor Ross, who was to be Jarrell's extremely talented student at Greensboro. The Peter Taylor issue of the *Shenandoah* (Winter, 1977) furnishes many details of the way their lives intertwined.[33] In a letter to me Robie Macauley remarked: "Peter always had the best perceptions about Randall of any of us—funny, analytical, and essentially, very sympathetic."[34]

When it became evident that Ransom was leaving Vanderbilt, the students chose Jarrell as their spokesman to present the petition of a delegation, which he headed, to the Chancellor, but the effort was useless. In 1937 John Crowe Ransom left for Kenyon College in Gambier, Ohio, and in 1938 Randall followed him. Peter Taylor, who went back to Memphis (Southwestern), became another pilgrim to Gambier the next year.

## IV    *At Kenyon as Instructor and Graduate Student*

Consisting of five hundred beautiful acres, Kenyon College, founded by the Episcopalian Church in 1824, was richly provided for by the English noblemen who gave it, as well as Gambier, their names; it is the sister-school of the university at Sewanee, Tennessee. When it burned to the ground in the late 1940s, it was rebuilt exactly as it had been. Were they to return, Randall and his group would miss none of the familiar spots, such as the Gothic Old Kenyon and Bexley Hall. Kenyon's traditions and spirit were all a small student body could wish for.

For the next two years Jarrell lived at Kenyon, teaching as he continued to work on his master's thesis, and after he had finished it. He rented accommodations at the Ransoms, where Robert Lowell also stayed. Lowell had never attended Vanderbilt: he came out from Harvard to Tennessee in April 1937, to study under Ransom (though he was a Classics, not an English, major) and, after two months of camping out on the Allen Tates' lawn at Clarksville, followed him to Gambier.[35] The two young poets became friends, remaining so till the last. In those days it was Tate who was closest to Lowell, but as he affirmed in 1963, later Jarrell took first place. If this friendship (unlike that between Jarrell and the non-poet Taylor) was marked by competition, this was only natural because of Lowell's winning the same honors and appointments, and in addition the Pulitzer Prize. As late as the year of Jarrell's death critic Roger Sale in the Summer *Hudson Review* (1965) called him a minor poet compared to Lowell (p. 309), an irritating and unwarranted dictum.

After Randall died, Robert ("Cal") Lowell wrote three elegies of sonnet length, dated October 1965, bringing readers as close to the young Jarrell as they are likely to come. He pictures the two of them at Kenyon:

> Thirty years ago,
> as students waiting for Europe and spring term to end—
> we saw below us, golden, small, stockstill, the college polo field, cornfields,
>     the feudal airdrome,
> the MacKinly Trust; behind, above us, the tower,
> the dorms, the fieldhouse, the Bishop's palace and chapel—

The second keeps on remembering, closing as did the initial sonnet with details, imagined, about the poet's death in a car accident. Lowell reconstructs their return once to the campus:

> coming back to Kenyon on the Ohio local—
> the view, middle distance, back and foreground, shifts,
> silos shifting squares like chessmen—a wheel
> turned by the water buffalo through the blue
> of true space before the dawn of days. . . .[36]

The affection running through these three sonnets, which grew from Kenyon days on, culminated in the following generous estimate when in 1963 Lowell was interviewed by Frederick Seidel for the *Paris Review:* "Jarrell's a great man of letters, a very well informed man, and the best critic of my generation, the best professional poet."[37] His own *The Mill of the Kavanaughs,* sometimes compared with Jarrell's work, is evidence of the respect he always had for his friend's reactions to his manuscripts.

A fellow townsman of Memphis-born Peter Taylor, David Mac-Dowell (long a publisher at Random House) was a student at the time in Gambier, the secretary of the young *Kenyon Review*. His recollection of Jarrell is of a formidable scholar, occasionally arrogant but with a pleasant side to him, like a child.[38] When they played tennis, the poet often won, to MacDowell's fury, knowing himself to be the better player. Wiry but not frail, Randall continued to love the sports he had enjoyed with Bernard Breyer and other Nashville friends: golf, touch football, badminton. As for spectator sports, he was, like Ransom, unapproachable during a football game; the year before his death he told the *Yale Daily News Reporter,* "The best thing I see on television are the pro-football games" (April 16, 1964).

After leaving the Ransom home, Jarrell was put in charge of a place which President Gordon "Rocky" Chalmers had secured for him and other Kenyonites (including Robie Macauley), the Douglass House, on the Middle Path in Gambier across from the old post office. One day MacDowell entered to find Randall sitting on the floor amidst strewn papers and exclaimed: "Great Scott, Randall, can I help straighten these things up?" Indignantly the poet refused, declaring that he understood his own ordering, that he knew every line he had ever written, and that some day five or six of his lyrics would be in all anthologies of world poetry.[39]

Taking his first step toward becoming "a bear," as he was to call himself, Jarrell during his Kenyon days grew a little moustache, with which he is represented in John Ciardi's *Five Young American Poets.* It concealed somewhat "the buck-toothed smile that gave him the look of one of Disney's amiable forest denizens—squirrel or beaver, maybe," as Bernard Breyer wrote me June 13, 1979. The undated "The Northern Snows" preserves details of campus life then—volleyball with Morey Lewis, (Taylor calls him Maury in the memorial volume, p. 245), skating, (perhaps in the new red wool shirt of "January 1938,") down to the Bishop's dam ("The Skaters"), skiing from the cemetery to the golf course. In the November 1954, *Harper's,* reviewing Arnold Toynbee, Jarrell reconstructs another side of his Kenyon College experience: "I began reading *A Study of History* on a cold, snowy, Ohio evening in the year 1937, and I've been reading it, off and on, ever since."

Despite an unhappy love affair ("In Those Days"), Kenyon was a good interlude for Jarrell, who reveled in his American Literature class in Ascension Hall despite its early-morning scheduling and in the clash of mind on mind that its gifted scholars afforded him, persons like John W. Thompson, poet and fiction writer and now chairman of English at Stony Brook, Long Island.

The poems Jarrell was then writing were not much different from those at Vanderbilt, such as "When Achilles fought and fell," "A Dialogue between soul and body," "Enormous Love, it's no use asking," "Falling in love is never as simple." These four, with their Audenesque ring, published in 1937, are representative of the Nashville era, and not too different from the verse of Allen Tate, who was to leave Tennessee for a post at Greensboro. "Old Poems," a sonnet of 1937, suggests a discarding of juvenilia, a practice Jarrell may have followed, while at the same time it rejects extensive revision in favor of letting a lyric reflect the exact time at which it was written, a point of view quite different from Auden's. A major step toward maturity for Randall Jarrell was "The Ways and the People," his first appearance in *Poetry* (July, 1939); it was reprinted in the magazine's sixtieth anniversary issue.

## V   *From Kenyon to the Armistice*

After receiving the Vanderbilt M.A., Jarrell was ready for job-hunting. Encouraged by his mother to continue the Ph.D., he announced he would wait for an honorary degree, as being cheaper

(Bard College in 1962 was to fulfill the prophecy). Randall's first position was at the University of Texas in Austin, where he taught from 1939 to 1942, continuing to search for his own idiom in poetry, one separate from the concrete/abstract idiosyncracies of Auden. In a civil ceremony in June 1940, he married Mackie Langham, his colleague on the English faculty, who was very well liked by Nashville friends and family when he took her home for a visit that same month. During the visit Randall's mother insisted on Mackie's calling her "Anne."

The prelude "under the Texas sun" to the Pearl Harbor catastrophe, was, on the whole, a quiet season for Jarrell. The young poet was as sports-conscious as ever: in a University of Wisconsin recording (2134) of his reading to an audience, Randall relates how he learned pitch (used in "Eighth Air Force") from the football players at Texas University when he used to teach there (the simplest game in the world "next to Animal Grab"). The years were productive in criticism and verse, culminating in the first volume (1942), *Blood for a Stranger.* Even before that, Jarrell had made his debut from the Texas campus with over forty pages of poems and prose in the above-mentioned *Five Young American Poets,* which New Directions brought out in 1940.

After the New Directions anthology Jarrell began to be noticed. How flattered he would have felt had he been able to read the letter that the eminent critic Edmund Wilson wrote to Cap Peace on December 20, 1940 ("Why don't you run some of Jarrell's poetry in the *New Yorker?* His writing interests me more, I think, than that of any of the other younger people. . . .") or the letter the same man sent to Morton Zabel the following year blaming Malcolm Cowley for not doing Jarrell justice in the *New Republic's* reviewing section.[40] Yet, strangely enough, his idol Ransom was not so laudatory when he appraised in the *Kenyon Review* these first poems printed by Ciardi. Even though he considered Jarrell the most brilliant of the five chosen poets, he blames him for "absurd near-rhymes and coy changes of pace," as well as obscure ellipses, although he softens the blow by sensing in the young man an individuality which had not as yet learned how to display itself.[41]

Back at Kenyon, Randall's friend Peter Taylor graduated in 1940 with an A.B. In the same year his first *Kenyon Review* poem appeared, more a valediction than a beginning, since his forte was to be fiction and drama. Like a magnet, their alma mater was to draw Taylor away from Greensboro in the years to come, for a stint as teacher. In the shadows of the coming war, his was to be a different choice from Lowell's in that he joined the forces, becoming a sergeant. It might not have differed from Randall's, had the latter passed basics. Randall had the heart of a pacifist, but a heart "lacerated with fierce indignation."

With the December 7, 1941, attack, Jarrell entered a ferry pilot training program in Austin, but, "washing out," automatically became a private in the Air Force. After basic training at Sheppard's Field in Wichitaw Falls, Texas, he was transferred to Canute Field, Rantoul, Illinois, and finally stationed at Davis-Monthan Field in Tucson for the duration of the war. At Tucson he served as an instructor of B-29 crewmen, the last years in Celestial Navigation, a role about as poetic as military possibilities allowed this lover of Orion and other constellations. Not only did he enjoy the actual teaching but the sense of belonging to something larger than himself, a body of men initiated into the precise technical terminology that *Little Friend, Little Friend* and *Losses*, with their notes, make much of.

As even the early "The Machine Gun" *(Blood for a Stranger)* shows, Jarrell's attitude towards the service was ambivalent. Its duties left him enough time to write literary criticism and poems, because his finances had been improved by Mackie's Red Cross job. Though he had to teach how to kill, he was spared the sight of killing except in his imagination. In February, 1946, he was discharged at San Antonio, a few months after the "false Armistice" he speaks about in the cassette *The Poet's Voice*, made at Harvard. A quarter of a century later, he could describe the war to young Schatzow at Yale as "a combination of 'Alice in Wonderland' and Dostoevsky's 'House of the Dead.'" Though the war experience formed a chapter of life far from easy for his conscience to assess, he saw it as to be endured for freedom, in a vision of "necessity" which for him, unlike Lowell, was anything but simple. "Second Air Force," during which a mother views the camp (possibly an autobiographical lyric), hints at how impossible oversimplifications were for either civilian or soldier.

## VI   *The Man Who Gladly Taught*

Once out of uniform, Jarrell returned to teaching English, this time at Sarah Lawrence College in New York City. He and Mackie saw a great deal of the Robie Macauleys there, and of the Peter Taylors, who had also migrated to New York. Like Wordsworth, he knew himself called to be a poet, but he also knew that he was a born teacher. Suzanne Ferguson feels that for Jarrell criticism and teaching were synonymous: "His critical writings were all teaching: teaching readers how to know and love Frost, Stevens, Williams, Marianne Moore, Whitman, Kipling, Lowell, and more; teaching the difference between good writing and bad writing, truth and falsehood; teaching his audience, directly and incidentally, to read all his own favorite writers by commanding, cajoling, dropping tempting allusions."[42] Even the poems extend his role as teacher, poems intimately written to a "few readers," as a lyrical understatement asserts, but actually to an ever-increasing readership, who looked to him for directions on how life should be lived, for warnings on how easily life can be missed.

In 1947, through the arrangements of Peter Taylor, who had begun teaching at the Women's College of the University of North Carolina in Greensboro, Randall and Mackie Jarrell joined the faculty there, under the chairmanship of Dr. Leonard Hurley, he as associate professor, she as instructor in composition and English literature. Peter and Randall had a joint seminar, the latter's part according to the catalog including Auden, Eliot, Dickinson, Hardy, Donne, Blake, Chekhov, Tolstoy, Melville, James, Dickens, Malraux, Empson, Blackmur, although in reality he never cared if he finished a textbook and might spend a week on a stanza, sometimes on a single line. Jarrell himself had had memorable teachers like Mary Louise Goodwin at Hume-Fogg and John Crowe Ransom, whose courtliness he may have been imitating when he closed each Greensboro class by rising and saying "Thank you very much."

The Jarrells settled at 1924 Spring Garden, a house they were to share with the Taylors. To this address came celebrities like Robert Frost, whenever the annual Arts Festival sponsored by the *Coraddi* (literary magazine) rolled around. Success seemed to arrive all of a sudden: a Guggenheim even before Greensboro, the appointment as acting poetry editor of *The Nation*, representation in Ciardi's anthology, and two books of his own (*Blood for a Stranger* and *Little Friend, Little Friend*). Later he won distinctions such as the Levinson Prize and the thousand-dollar award given by the National Institute of Arts and Letters. He frequently contributed to the "Big Four" reviews (*Kenyon, Hudson, Sewanee, Partisan*), serving as poetry reviewer in the last-named. *Losses* and *The Seven-League Crutches* appeared. There were absences from Greensboro, the 1948 summer seminar in American Civilization at Salzburg, which he attended alone, stopping in Paris on the way back, and the visiting professorship at Princeton (1951–52), where he held seminars in literary criticism, but Greensboro had become home, more so than California had been and in a different way from Tennessee.

By 1951, he and Mackie had decided to separate, getting a divorce the following year. In November 1952, he married Mary von Schrader, whom he had met when she entered his Creative Writing seminar in Boulder, Colorado.

Robie Macauley, his and Taylor's old comrade from Kenyon, arrived in Greensboro in 1950 to become a welcome third to the seminar that fall. (In 1953 Macauley left with his wife for Washington.) Randall confined himself to the poetry part. When the Jarrells moved to the University of Illinois campus in Urbana for a semester in the early 1950s, Robert Watson, fresh from the Johns Hopkins doctoral program, began to teach on the Greensboro campus, where he became Randall's trusted and understanding friend.

In 1953 *Poetry and the Age* came out. Those who read it with amusement (even astonishment) at its apothegms, recognized that something new was stirring in criticism, a "happening" on Olympus, an approach quite different from that of the New Critics, who had held sway in the United States during most of the century. In quite another literary direction, *The Gingerbread Rabbit* and *The Bat-Poet* appeared, done by the child Jarrell for children of all ages.

Flannery O'Connor, who had not thought much of *Pictures from an Institution*, was a March 1955, *Coraddi* festival guest, and in her inimitable style has left a glimpse of the Jarrell household in a letter to the Fitzgeralds after her return to Milledgeville; she feels she said nothing intelligent while in Greensboro but seems to have taken away some good memories:

Mr. Randall Jarrell, wife and stepdaughters I met and et dinner with. I must say I was shocked at what a very kind man he is—that is the last impression I expected to have of him. I also met Peter Taylor, who is more like folks. Mrs. Jarrell is writing a novel. You get the impression the two stepdaughters may be at it too and maybe the dog. Mr. Jarrell has a beard and looks like Mephistopheles (sp?) only fatter. Mrs. Jarrell is very friendly & sunkist.

Jarrell was indeed quite different from the picture she had had of him in her December 26, 1954, letter to Sally Fitzgerald telling her of the Arts Festival invitation in Greensboro, "where Brother Randall Jarrell holds forth: 'I accepted but I am not looking forward to it. Can you imagine me hung in conversation with the likes of him?'"[43]

The young women studying under Jarrell thought of him possessively as their poet laureate, who quickened their abilities through seminars, small-group discussions, readings, conferences. Several went on to achieve writing careers of their own, women such as Emily Herring Wilson, whom A. M. Ammons describes as one of the best poets of the South, her poems "stations where we can pause, and coming to know the self of and in the poem, learn ourselves."[44] They took pride in his Sendak-illustrated books, his chancellorship of the Academy of American Poets, and his poetry editorship of the *Yale Review*, a responsibility which kept him speeding to the mailbox with scores of reviews. They were thrilled at the sight of him behind the wheel of his sports car, as photographed by Philippe Halsman for the *Saturday Evening Post* article "The Appalling Taste of the Age."[45] The Mercedes-Benz, giving him a power he had seen in the S-F scientists of his childhood passion which never left him, was symbolic: "Cars are some of the things we share with the rest of the world, the rest of the ages: a man polishing his Mercedes is the last link in a chain that goes back to Achilles, patting his divine steeds Balius and Xanthus or, at least, that's what I tell myself as I polish my Mercedes."[46]

Reluctantly, the Women's College accepted his absence during the two-year consultantship in poetry at the Library of Congress in 1956–1958. He liked living in the Nation's capital, with Mary and her two daughters by a previous marriage, Alleyne and Beatrice: the easy work in the office, the[47] leisure activities including trips to the Rock Creek Park Zoo (the "canyons" of which reminded him of a heavily forested California area), gallery-going, and baseball games. Mary and Randall Jarrell saw a lot of the Macauleys, as he and Mackie had at Sarah Lawrence. When he returned to Greensboro, he found himself working with George Murray Nauss, instead of Taylor and Macaulay in the seminar. Nauss had in the interim joined the faculty from the University of Iowa.

At the Vanderbilt Spring Symposium of 1961, the Randall Jarrell who participated was quite different from the "angry young man" who had figuratively stomped out of Nashville to Gambier after his favorite teacher, Ransom. Bearded and handsome, with perfect grooming and taste in clothes, he had become the Gentleman Scholar, a teacher and poet with an ever-widening circle of influence. That his reputation advanced was partly due to a series of paperbacks he edited for Doubleday but more to the acclaim that greeted *The Woman at the Washington Zoo*, a National Book Award winner which drew over a thousand to celebrate in his honor at Chapel Hill. To the tributes, Jarrell responded simply: "I don't know what to say." The newspaper

editor Sam Ragan remembers seeing on that occasion a like simplicity
in Mary and Randall skipping hand in hand over the Chapel Hill
grounds.[48] In Greensboro the first issue of the short-lived literary magazine *Analects* was dedicated to him.

As pictured in the school annual *Pine Needles*, lying in his hammock
on South Lake Drive in 1961, he translated Rilke, Grimm, Beckstein.
Jarrell seemed on the top of the wheel of fortune, yet *A Sad Heart at
the Supermarket* was in some ways a disquieting book, written by a
person not at ease within himself. The honors continued: another Guggenheim; the honorary degree from Bard College at Annandale-on-
Hudson; the Actors' Studio production of his *The Three Sisters,* which
he and Mary attended in June of 1964 in New York; an evening lecture
prefaced by an afternoon reading on October 24, 1962, at the National
Poetry Festival. But there were the dry seasons when his poetry threatened to stop. Moreover, he was concerned about his mother, who, after
moving from apartment to apartment and trying to take care of her
failing sister, Mary Anne, had entered a nursing home in Nashville.[49]

The last twelve months of his life (1964–1965) were the hardest.
Their difficulty climaxed in a period of hospitalization in Chapel Hill
from February till May as the result of a mental breakdown. By fall he
was able to resume his classes: Russian literature in translation and the
poetry sessions. Kelly Cherry, artist-in-residence at the University of
Wisconsin in Madison now, remembers him in the poetry class she
audited as someone who enjoyed his role: the old enthusiasm had not
gone.

A few months before the publication of that lifetime of memories
entitled *The Lost World,* Randall Jarrell was struck by a car on October 24, 1965, on the Jefferson-Davis Highway 13 outside Chapel Hill.
He was killed instantly (a skull fracture), his body unmutilated.[50] The
funeral was an Episcopalian service in Greensboro on October 17, with
interment in the New Garden Friends Cemetery in Guilford, not far
from the Jarrell home.

So ended that half-century allotted to Jarrell. He never got the
chance to say, like the cartwright in Changtse, who spent a long life
learning his craft, "Therefore, at the age of seventy, I am good at making wheels."[51] But to deny him the title of major writer would be to
deny the cosmos he constructed out of his "very rich hours," brief
though they were, on this marvelous planet, Earth.

### CHAPTER 2

# Wingless Airman: The War Years

IN reviewing the poetic legacy left by Randall Jarrell I have chosen the method of carefully examining a few specimens of selected genres: as his friend Robert Frost says, "All an artist needs is samples." Although the war poems were an interruption, a tale he felt he had to tell, written in the blood of strangers who were not strangers but brothers, it is for these that he first became widely known. Though never overseas himself, he must have known well during his four years in the Air Force many young pilots later listed as casualties. The discharge from his instructorship as Celestial Navagation tower operator came in 1946, a year after the publication of *Little Friend, Little Friend* and two years before that of *Losses*. Few of the war lyrics in these are set in the Southwest where he was stationed, "Leave," "Transient Barracks," and "Second Air Force" being some exceptions. Not only fighters abroad but also the wounded, the imprisoned, the veterans, civilians who suffered through the severance of relationships became part of the record that has earned for him the title of America's foremost poet of World War II.

## I "Burning the Letters"

"The war poems," writes critic John Fuller about Randall Jarrell, "show a public hell, an individual dream, in imaginative and concrete equation."[1] The "public hell" comes through as a discordant obligato in one of the most difficult Jarrell monologues, "Burning the Letters." Although the mourner here is particular, a woman who after years of clinging to memories frees herself from a sterile grief, the experience is general, or "public." The decapitation of the corpse she never saw, with the head "charred, featureless," is but an exemplum of other husbands' mutilation as carriers were plunged to the bottom of the Pacific or planes exploded. Fuller's "individual dream" sometimes takes the form of soldiers trying to escape in dreams the nightmare of battle; what Crusoe says in "The Islands" is true of each, prematurely aged

41

and unable to believe that their homes in the United States still exist:
"I have dreamed of men, and I am old./ There is no Europe." At other
times it encompasses both waking hours and sleep: the sentence *Es war
ein Traum*, occurs in "1914," (Jarrell's one prose-poem), written
beneath the photograph of a World War I soldier, taken months after
he has been killed: "It [life, death, war] is the dream from which no
one wakes."

One reason for the obscurity of "Burning the Letters" is that Jarrell
in the interior monologue assumes the woman's identity by adopting
the first person singular, whereas "The Woman at the Washington
Zoo," "Lady Bates," "A Girl in a Library," and other lyrics which center on women present the poet as narrator. Yet only the first and last
parts can possibly be imagined as the thoughts of the widow as she
burns the letters, even granted the conventions of verse. The middle
section with its convoluted religious paradoxes seems dramatically
unjustified. If the title, "Burning the Letters," signifies the primary
meaning of the poem, its secondary sense (the dying of her Christian
faith, a level underscored by the headnote referring to her as formerly
a Protestant Christian) might have emerged more effectively had a
third-person narration obtained throughout, or had her own conscious-
ness been kept the focus.

"Burning the Letters" uses as stage for the horrors of war experienced indirectly the mind of a pilot's widow, who seeks release from
a sorrow which has held her prisoner since the arrival of the death-
message years before. As it opens, she addresses her forever-young husband, whose "unchanged self" has lived within her, just as she did
within him when as he flew his missions she remained his "one
unchanging country." While he stays the same as in the yellowed
newspaper photograph, she, bound by the laws of time, grows gray. In
her imagination she reconstructs the bombing she never saw: the
flames rising from the sea, the carrier and planes engulfed, the bodies
gathered up by those designated to weight them for burial.

The first seven lines show the moving pictures that have lived within
her since the war: her husband as she last saw him (real), the circumstances of his death (imagined):

> Here in my head, the home that is left for you,
> You have not changed; the flames rise from the sea
> And the sea changes; the carrier, torn in two,
> Sinks to its planes—the corpses of the carrier

> Are strewn like ashes on the star-reflecting sea;
> Are gathered, sewn with weights, are sunk.
> The gatherers disperse.

The lines are connected by Jarrell's technique of bringing down one word into the following line (*you . . . you; sea . . . sea; carrier . . . carrier;* another use of *sea* relating back to the second and third lines; *gathered . . . gatherers*'). If one were to think of these repetitions as printed in red type, they would be as so many drops of blood splattered across the text.

With the second paragraph the rhythm roughens, though still basically pentameter, imitative of the woman's disturbed condition as she kneels or sits before the fireplace in her lonely dwelling. Another technical device usual in Jarrell, substitution, is employed: while the woman is holding out the as-yet-unburned correspondence figuratively washed up to her by the ocean, the expression "Here in my head" of the opening becomes "Here in my hands." As she received these letters, she replied to their questions, the questions that asked so much and so little at the same time, realizing as she read each one how she was the force enabling her man to survive. Now, after years and years have accumulated, it is as if the answers she sent back had been written by someone other than herself, a friend of the wife and cat who stayed at home waiting for the soldier and eventually died, even as he died, in the lyric surviving their decease. Therefore, the sheets she is burning are letters written not to her but to a ghost. She herself is newborn, a believer in death at last, like the "ear that listens to the owl" in "The Bird of Night." But she has also learned how to believe again in the dailiness of a life lived in terms of *my* and *I*, not *we* and *our*.

This sort of paraphrase gives the reader her outer and inner experience but does not lead deeply enough into Jarrell's poem. The metaphysical nucleus begins to radiate out in the seascape of the ninth line, "the sea's dark, incalculable calm," reminiscent of Wallace Stevens. The whole meditation revolves around change, that mysterious word put all in capitals in the last verse of "Children Selecting Books in a Library": "CHANGE, dear to all things not to themselves endeared." Change represents what she wants, what the woman at the Washington Zoo wants, what we all long for in our pursuit of joy that I have taken up in regard to Randall Jarrell in *The Metamorphic Tradition in Modern Poetry*.[2]

Though "The unchanging circle of the universe" follows "the sea's dark, incalculable calm," these are separate, not in apposition, since, above, the sea has been termed changing, again a concept recalling Stevens. As the letters burn, her eyes, now dewy-eyed with sad recollections, like—CHANGE's ("dewy-eyed") in "Children Selecting Books," follow the flames of the past bombing. The dancing and glimmering of the real flames in the fireplace become one with "the hunting wings of the light" (the destroyed fighter plane). In the pre-Vatican II Mass, the Preface of the Requiem service contains the words "Life is changed, not taken away"; so it is with this woman's life as the two sets of flames merge into a single fire.

The burning of the letters is presented throughout the poem as a religious ritual, relying upon the given-up Christianity for its vocabulary. In her youth the woman possessed faith but it was only a child's, which did not mature along with her physical being; it remained like the husband's life "a child's eternally." When the woman looks back at her childhood she sees once more and reacts against the "savage figures" of the Crucifixion.

Though Jarrell's headnote and the lyric itself show her as a person who no longer adheres to Christianity, the paradoxes of death and life as embodied in the Passion-Resurrection event elicit from her a kind of unorthodox faith rather than complete disbelief. The Eucharistic reference to "the dark, veined bread/ Later than all law"—one of Jarrell's many uses of the image of blood, to which he was drawn while at the same time repulsed by any sight of blood—implies that the liturgy of Christ has superseded the legalism of Moses. Christ as scapegoat is implied throughout the poem: Parker Tyler puts this aspect well in "We witness the haunting pervasiveness of the scapegoat image for Mr. Jarrell in that so distinctively moving poem—swept by the tragedy of the commonplace—*Burning the Letters*."[3] She thinks:

> Men's one life issues, neither out of earth
> Nor from the sea, the last dissolving sea,
> But out of death: by man came death
> And his Life wells from death, the death of Man.

Jarrell's capitals are never arbitrary: why should *Life* and *Man* here receive capitals if they have no spiritual significance? Further on, it is hard to understand what *Light* means in "The Light flames, flushing the passive face/ With its eternal life," unless it means the Light of the world, Christ, though on the other hand the capitalized noun may be a deification of fire itself, purifying her and taking away all useless regrets. Yet it is the Sixth Word spoken from the Cross, "Consummatum est," that she borrows for the statement of her own victory: "It is finished." In any case, she has received absolution: the memories of her lost husband are at last only fragments, no fragments to be shored against ruin but ashes to be thrown into the grave of her past.[4]

## II  *"Eighth Air Force"*

Randall Jarrell, who insisted as early as *Mid-Century American Poets* that all of his lyrics were intended to be read aloud, would be particularly pleased that his reading of the war poem he himself preferred among his own, "Eighth Air Force," is available to anyone who visits the University of Wisconsin library and asks for Tape 2134: the recorded poem, of course, is procurable from many other sources. After a most amusing beginning before an unnamed audience, concerning the use to which he can finally put the customary glass of water (pills for the cold he then had) and the unlikely comparison he had recently heard of him and Tennyson, he identifies unfamiliar terms in "Transient Barracks," a selection based upon his Arizona experiences, and reads that poem; then goes on to a greater one.

Part of the horror in this second, "Eighth Air Force," set to flowers and music, is that the efficiency of the Eighth Air Force, responsible for destroying the production centers of Germany, requires the "necessary" destruction of civilians along with railroads and factories. The poem is built on what Jarrell calls a Roman proverb: "Man is a wolf to man." The stage direction of Shakespeare, "Enter other murderer," seems applicable, as the fighters return. The monosyllable that the sweating pilot keeps repeating as if a clock were striking is given a specificity when Jarrell tells us that the man has flown twenty-four missions and is superstitiously fearing he will never make the required twenty-five. In the mounting nervousness of the approach to their release, many soldiers had just that reaction. To share in the commentary that precedes Jarrell's wonderfully expressive rendition of this brief but deep war poem is to feel as he himself, who never went to any overseas camp, must have felt often: "You Are There."

George W. Nitchie ranks "Burning the Letters" very high in the category of Jarrell's war poems: it seems to him, along "with Lowell's 'The Quaker Graveyard in Nantucket' and Yeats's 'In Memory of Major Robert Gregory,' one of the great elegies of our century, perhaps

of any century."[5] But "Eighth Air Force" is more than an elegy of one
soldier, or even of one segment of the army, that assigned to bomb
Germany from England: it is an elegy for, and at the same time an
exoneration of, all the American combatants. It begins with a question
as to the justice of attributing total guilt to the pilots waiting in a troop
station for their next mission:

> If, in an odd angle of the hutment,
> A puppy laps the water from a can
> Of flowers, and the drunk sergeant shaving
> Whistles *O Paradiso!*—shall I say that man
> Is not as men have said, a wolf to man?

"Hutment," as the English say, is a collection of huts, the encampment
itself looked at here from an "odd angle," one not destined for the
history books but even so part of history.

The four five-line stanzas keep to identical rhyme (*man* being
employed so six times) for their chief patterning device, with end-var-
iations of perfect (*can*) and oblique (*one*) rhymes. This repetition of
*man*, with its theistic overtones despite the absence of capitalization,
unites the poem to "Burning the Letters." The scene of these soldiers
getting ready for another day is no different from the routine back in
the Arizona barracks, and the men themselves not really any more like
wolves than they were then, as shown by the comparison to the puppy
who laps water from a can of flowers. In another poem, "Second Air
Force," the crew members climbing into their planes are dehumanized
into bears, an approximation of wolves, in contrast to the puppy here.
The gathering of these blossoms, stuck in their makeshift container,
reminiscent of civilian days, like the japonica outside the camp window
in Henry Reed's "The Naming of Parts," fits in with the operatic air
(an aria from Act III of Meyerbeer's *L'Africaine*) whistled by the shav-
ing sergeant and, like the liquor which has made him drunk, is a way
of deadening consciences as well as the pain of dislocation from home.

The poet, who has assumed the role of judge (Pilate), is not willing
to remit their sins of savagery without qualification, as his stress on the
nonchalance of the returning murderers implies. The weary bomba-
diers come back from their night raids to the camp yawning, ready to
relax in a game of pitch or to sleep. Only one of the five lies in a sweat
of fear, counting the missions between Now (Europe) and Soon (America). Lawrence Noriega, in his University of Virginia doctoral disser-

tation[6] on Randall Jarrell, writes about this fifth, in a letter to the author (December, 1977): "The one who is on the bunk counting missions with the passionate and reduced simplicity of one—one, one is so beautifully supported by the almost blunt facility of 'Still, this is how it's done.'"

"Eighth Air Force" makes clear that the "odd angle" from which the knot of murderers is viewed is that of Pontius Pilate facing the Son of Man on the morning of the Crucifixion, here Jarrell's own "mask" as he wrestles with the moral problem his friend Lowell had solved by conscientious objection, leading to prison for him. In the fairy tales, it is easy enough to tell villain from hero: the wicked witch who burns to death miserably in *Hansel and Gretel* deserves her fate. But in real life good and evil are not discrete; thus the ordinary typeface "murderers" in the second stanza becomes "*O murderers!*" in its last line, the change to italics prefaced by a moan and followed by an exclamation point.

The rest of the lyric telescopes the men into a single figure, standing before the judgment seat of Pilate, who feels himself one of them in that he too is a man. When the war broke out, the Allies gave as their motivation saving the world so that freedom, peace, culture, all that was best in Western tradition, could survive. The means of doing so, Pilate decides as he speaks his *Ecce Homo*, must be the death of this composite man, the "last saviour," over which the poet has suffered "in a dream" (life mirrored in his art).

Only three of the twenty lines here are in regular iambic pentameter, such as the balanced "I did as these have done, but did not die," Jarrell's and Pilate's self-incrimination. Three juxtaposed strong beats are the dominant prosodic feature ("This is a war. . . . But since these play, before they die"), mounting to five in the portrayal of the frightened airman's anxiety: "Till even his heart beats: One; One; One."[7] The most ingenious stroke is "I find no fault in this just man," since *just* can be taken in the sense of the fighters being "merely" human. Pilate's "What is truth?" becomes " . . . what is lying?" Like Odysseus, Jarrell has used the artistic "lie" to tell the deepest truth.

### III  *Some Other War Lyrics*

During the years at Vanderbilt, Jarrell was daily confronted with the R.O.T.C. building, a prominent feature on the campus representing the high prestige of military service in its program as at the nearby

University of the South in Sewanee, where two Jarrells are listed on the
tablets of war heroes and another Jarrell until recently was on the military science faculty. A soldier's life, as the poet came to know it in
Texas, seemed far from heroic, a stepping out of civilian individuality
into a realm of dog tags and other forms of de-personalization, even to
the public receiving of mail. Like "Say Good-bye to Big Daddy," Jarrell's "Mail Call" rarely fails to impress college students. The setting
could be either abroad or in boot camp. Though its economy skips
direct mention of a mail sergeant's tossing out letters as he reads aloud
addressees, the first line creates that picture: "The letters always just
evade the hand." If Archibald MacLeish's combination of "empty
doorway" and "yellow maple leaf" constitutes an objective correlative
for loneliness, so do the letters falling like stones or birds into hands
other than those of the man who "wishes simply for his name." The
recruiting slogan "Join the Navy and See the World" twists ironically
into the outcome of enlistment: "In letters and in dreams they see the
world."

Another externally quiet episode is that interval of peacefulness, the
furlough, wherein "The Soldier Walks under the Trees of the University." The institution might be Nashville's Vanderbilt, another university of the South, or a composite like the background in *The Animal
Family*. A strict confinement to four stanzas of eight lines each ema-
nates an effect of private order within general disorder. Jarrell's love
of trees becomes exaltation in the Yeatsian "green magnificence of
these great lives," the shade of which darkens brick walls. This
"unwalled world" is completely unlike that other one to which the soldier must return, a desert-camp world unprotected by walls of trees
and overshadowed by the darkness of combats to come, strife which
these leisurely or hurrying collegians cannot visualize: they are only
"pupils," a noun signifying both students and eyes, shining here like
flowers in their groves of academic tranquillity.

The name of Vanderbilt, Jarrell's alma mater, fits in with "In our
zone innocence is born in banks/ And cultured in colonies the rich
have sown." While not obsessed with *usura* and its consequences, Jarrell was quite aware of the connection between money-lending and
war. He also knew how old professors write the histories that young
men live, safe "oaks" writing of broken "reeds." (*"The oak escapes the
storm that broke the reeds."*) Around each such oak is the Chekhovian
gold chain. If the lyric is autobiographical, it was only a short while
ago that its writer was also an ignorant reader of the pain in others'

lives, lives as remote from his own as were the names of cities over which his comrades in service were slated to die, though as boys they had not known of the existence of these cities. "The Märchen" shows that books *can* teach about life, yet "We" in stanza three seems a bitter self-reproach for Jarrell's former blindness in relegating the poor, guilt, death, evil, to neat enclaves where print substitutes for blood and pseudo-patience for suffering. The repetition "in books, in books, in books" is a breast-beating.

The last stanza of "The Soldier Walks ...", impassioned yet restrained, is one of the most beautiful in Randall Jarrell:

> When will the boughs break blazing from these trees,
> The darkened walls float heavenward like soot?
> The days when men say: "Where we look is fire—
> The iron branches flower in my veins"?
> In that night even to be rich is difficult,
> The world is something even books believe,
> The bombs fall all year long among the states,
> And the blood is black upon the upturned leaves.

Also derived from flight-instructor Jarrell's indirect contact with the conflagration making red the skies of both hemispheres is "The Rising Sun," inspired by a film shown as part of the soldiers' training at the Arizona base. Though never in the Orient himself, Jarrell skillfully incorporates symbolic details from the film on Japan: the bowing, rice marshes, snow and its "spring-time sister," petals. Through hallucination the poet identifies with a child on the enemy's side, a four-year-old in the Empire of the Rising Sun. Unlike the sick child in "A Quilt-Pattern," who builds a card-house on his coverlet, this boy really lives in a flimsy card-house, at the mercy of the earthquake tremors that are frequent in Japan. Whether in a dream, an actual quake from a geological fault under the house, or a bombing, his mother rushes to him in that superlative devotion to children characteristic of Japanese maternity.

Without the notes to *Selected Poems* the lyric would be indefensible against a charge of obscurity, no matter what Jarrell had to say to his Harvard audience in disparagement of those who find modern poetry difficult. But these do exist, and so the surrealistic insertion about the five-colored cloud becomes as clear as dream requires with the information that it refers to one such cloud seen by a palace official and

made the occasion of an imperial decree for a festival. There is no
reason not to take at face value and work out from there the poet's
own assertion that he has in mind the memorial service in a temple
after a Japanese soldier's ashes have been shipped home, the mourners
gathered to witness the puff of a ceremonial cigarette in honor of the
"weak ghost." This "child" who later died awakened from a dream
midway through the lyric (line 18); the mourners now awake, after his
deliverance to them by the Deliverer, War, though it is from the child's
dream, his own life, that they awake.

When "The Rising Sun," first appearing in Ransom's *Kenyon
Review* the spring before, was annotated in 1948 for *Losses*, Jarrell
wrote: "I have said nothing, in these notes, about the wooden pillows,
fish-kites, dwarfed trees, and other familiar Japanese properties of the
poem. There is no need to search them for hidden meanings." The
tragedy of the ironic title suffices.

In "Second Air Force," a mother visits her soldier son and arrives to
find his environment an amalgam of sand roads, tar-paper barracks,
runways of bubbling asphalt, sage, dunes rising to the ranges over
which planes move from cloud to cloud—a landscape matching her
mood of desolation. The Fortresses await their masters like dragons
standing awkwardly on legs too small for their lifeless bodies; into these
"green made beasts" crawl the intelligent beings who will direct the
destruction they were invented for, boys who have been turned to
bears. Here, in "Transient Barracks," a black soldier returns to this
bomber training command, the Second Air Force, unspeakably grateful, as he shaves, for routine after the horrible bloodshed overseas. No
mention of a joyful reunion brightens the poem. The next stanza shows
mother and son standing together, in a forest of shadows, near the
hangar-hills buried under the "owl's air" of imminent death which also
washes the forest of "The Bird of Night." She has the feeling that she
and he are already drowned.

The pilots above are so caught up in operating their B-29s ("But for
them the bombers answer everything"), so full of the pride of life
which makes of every death the catastrophe of someone else, that they
cannot enter into their situation with the insight of this spectator. They
are, after all, just children, as Jarrell's soldiers inevitably are. The one
next to her was once in her womb, a part of her flesh; was the preg-
nancy only a prelude to flames eating along the steel wings till they
reach him within her as rib by rib they seek her heart?

One of my own favorites among the war poems is "Losses,"[8] touching in its accent on the youthfulness, the bewilderment of the fighters.

But the example that can scarcely be omitted in any treatment of Jarrell war lyrics is "The Death of the Ball Turret Gunner," which Douglas Dunn considers "perhaps the most famous of all Second World War poems," one which has about it "the indignation of acceptance."[9] Washing out garbage cans with a hose during K.P. duty in Arizona was the genesis for this frightening exclamation point to atrocity, which the publisher David Lewis brought out in a fine edition in 1969, with hand-colored designs by Robert Andrew Parker. The "child" in the airship is born not to life but to death. Seldom has so much meaning been compressed into five lines, with two rhymes, *froze* and *hose,* a chilling and inhuman condensation of the fate suffered by the pilot, of whom not even enough remained to need the "body bag" used after air crashes.

The State has become a grim stepmother to the gunner. The second line returns to the child as Admiral Byrd, of "90 North," standing in his dream at the North Pole in snow-wet furs while his "real" little body is hunched under the covers, just as the embryonic bomber's is hunched in the State's womb. The earth itself is the dreamer in the war poem, its dream ratifying Prospero's assertion in *The Tempest;* broken away from it as a parachute-jumper from the plane, the speaker has awakened to nightmare. The impersonal *they* in the last line ("When I died they washed me out of the turret with a hose") gathers up into four letters the horror of modern combat, the opposite of Trojan/Greek heroism in "When Achilles fought and fell." [10]

## IV  *What the War Meant to the "Wingless Airman"*

George W. Nitchie, who like Jarrell survived his time of service in the war without ever having to kill, in explaining why Randall was so unquestionably "the" poet of World War II, has this to say: "He drew, not on something like Owen's trench experience, but on something like Keats's negative capability."[11] He had the "aesthetic distance" to make others' sorrows his own, but this detachment in space from carnage would never have resulted in the large number of war lyrics he wrote before 1950 had he not felt himself a self-elected laureate for victim and survivor of that Strife which seemed for a time the force behind the movement of the sun and the other stars. To the inarticulate actors in air raids Jarrell served as voice; to his fellow-poets who found themselves in the midst of the killing he was a model, a deeply directive influence. W. D. Snodgrass begins his *Heart's Needle* with poems about his own experience in the war; thirty years later he affirmed that it was to Jarrell he had turned to learn how to express his emotions arising from the war.

Interpreted in the largest sense—and Randall Jarrell's lyrics are always stratified—the woman in "Burning the Letters" stands in synecdoche to bereaved Womanhood. Since there is no alternative she accepts death and widowhood, choosing over these a third and separate pain, a life of stoicism. The individualized aspect of her fate is starkly put by Suzanne Ferguson in *The Poetry of Randall Jarrell:* "She achieves freedom, but the price is dreadful to contemplate" (p. 83). The flames have become a savior, but with talons, Christ the fierce Eagle in this microcosmic metaphor of wifely agony. In like manner, through the noun *Man,* synecdoche informs "Eighth Air Force." The basis for the figure of speech is deeply felt, just the opposite from what Jarrell accuses a novelist of in an omnibus *Harper's* review: "A man, to Marquand, is a nexus of institutions, the half-unwilling, half-imaginary point at which Harvard, the Stock Exchange, and the Army intersect."[12]

The section headings within *The Complete Poems* show a breadth of involvement not bounded by Jarrell's restriction to American soil during the war's progress: "Bombers," "The Carrier," "Prisoners," "Children and Civilians," "Soldiers." That he should be considered a war poet is an oddity of twentieth-century history: no one could have been less suited for soldiery than this "lark for whom circumstances made war an inescapable concern; his poems of war are a necessary description and rejection," writes Douglas Dunn in "An Affable Misery." Just as single-minded indignation led Lowell into pacificism, a complex morality led Jarrell into military service.[13] The fact that his camp was in a desert dramatizes the polarization that went on within him. In World War I, Alan Seeger, noted today only for his "I Have a Rendezvous with Death," chose the keeping of promises as he saw them over the comforts of peace; he was one of that war's casualties. Randall Jarrell survived, to become the spokesman for the lost.

The war years remain a riddle tellingly summed up in the last words of *The Complete Poems:* "'I don't know.'" With peace, Jarrell returned to the pursuits and themes of peace, grateful to be "absent with official leave" from the hostilities ended by the Armistice. No more poignant coda can be offered to these four years than the three words closing his title-page epigraph to *Little Friend, Little Friend,* as the bomber calls in the soldier: "'Let's go home.'"

CHAPTER 3

# Girls and Angels: Two Lyrics Compared

B ESIDES being the poet of World War II, Randall Jarrell could be called the poet of the young, or again the poet of women, the last two aspects unite in his exhortations to "A Girl in a Library" and "Lady Bates," exegeses of which comprise this chapter. That he had an exceptional ability to see the lives of others from the inside is more true of his Tiresian assumptions of the feminine sex than when he wrote from the stance of his own, a fact rounding into universality that entrance into the human heart in the crisis of warfare achieved by the "wingless airman."

Though a lover of children, as they were of him, he never had any of his own. His paternal instinct knew a degree of fulfillment in his contact with the two small daughters that his second wife brought into their marriage in 1952. Beatrice especially, the younger, was a joy to him that increased with the years but also a source of pain when she married a physicist from Germany and left the family circle at Greensboro. Jarrell was not one of those about whom E. E. Cummings writes "and down they forgot as up they grew"; on the contrary, he kept and as artist re-created both the child's life of fantasy, as in "The Black Swan," and of actuality, as in the moving "Moving," even venturing into the subconscious ("The Girl Dreams That She Is Giselle"[1]) or his last exquisite narrative for children, *Fly by Night*, with its imaginative and comic title.

Despite the disclaimer of the label Southerner, Jarrell has a right to the noun, as native of Tennessee, longtime resident in North Carolina, teacher in Texas and soldier-instructor in the Air Force in Arizona. The head librarian at Virginia Wesleyan College in Norfolk, Virginia, Roland Nicholson, recalled vividly, in an interview of April 1, 1978, not only Jarrell's humor and the feeling he brought to reading his poetry, but his Southern accent which records preserve: "you-all" is a Southernism, whereas his "sumpin'" is neither Northern or Southern but, surprisingly, characteristic of this careful speaker. In his associa-

53

tion with blacks he enjoyed a warm personalism quite unlike that per-
mitted by a Northern setting to Wallace Stevens, whose "Decorations
in a Nigger Cemetery" reveals such insensitivity in its title that no
amount of sophisticated literary criticism can render the name of the
lyric acceptable.

Randall Jarrell's elegy on the black football star of the Baltimore
Colts, Lipscomb, "Say Good-bye to Big Daddy," affects college students in a manner totally different from any other contemporary
poem: at a 1970 summer institute in linguistics held at what was then
Norfolk State College a professor-lecturer from Penn State University
remarked of this phenomenon: "After Jarrell's death, the kids really
'went out' over that poem." In the paradoxical alternatives that conclude it ("The world won't be the same without Big Daddy/ Or else
it will be") one senses a premature lament for himself, even as Milton's
for King in "Lycidas" was for Milton. One reacts with incredulity to
Robert Weisberg's condemnation of the subject: "Who but Jarrell
would write a poem to a professional football player?"[2] a question
which need not have been pejorative were it not followed by blame of
Jarrell's "interest in mundane things like football," on the next page of
Weisberg's article. So much for Blake's grain of sand!

The Southern girls used as "samples" in this chapter are the child
Lady Bates and the student immortalized, at least in type, by "A Girl
in a Library." Both lyrics incorporate angels, one of the persistent
strands of imagery uniting the items in the Jarrell poetic corpus.

## I   *"Lady Bates"*

"Lady Bates" is an elegy for a Negro who was as "inglorious," in
Gray's phrase, as Big Daddy Lipscomb was famous. She died as a child,
before she could have the opportunity to be a student in the college
courses in Greensboro which Jarrell once declared he would pay to
teach, were he a rich man, so exhilarating did he find his profession.
Yet had Lady Bates lived, nothing but a miracle would have gained
her admittance among the lucky young women in Greensboro who
studied under Randall Jarrell. Jarrell's former student, Ann Vernon
(now Director of Tours at the Chrysler Museum in Norfolk, Virginia),
remembers how she was ostracized by both faculty and students at the
Women's College when she joined those protesting discrimination by
participating in the lunch-counter sit-ins in Greensboro in the early
1960s; she also recalls with gratitude how—when her very residency
on campus was threatened among many signs of hostility such as "lost"

mail—Randall Jarrell and his wife Mary offered her their home, should she need it.

Though Lady Bates's story is imagined, not historical (as, to a degree, was the story of Nestus Gurley, the Greensboro paperboy), Jarrell must have known many Lady Bateses in his Nashville boyhood as well as during his undergraduate career at Vanderbilt. His admired mentor among the English faculty there, John Crowe Ransom, may have supplied a model of sorts in "Bells for John Whiteside's Daughter," different as are the elegies of the two children. Both are apostrophes to the dead, working in flashbacks of action to heighten the pathos of the fatal repose with which each ends. Later, during his service at the Library of Congress in Washington, D.C., a city where Caucasians are in the minority, Jarrell appreciated the enjoyment of life and the humor of the black teen-agers who played about the baseball park. The *New York Times* for September 16, 1956, quotes his anecdote about this area:

"I stopped at one light, and a little boy shouted 'Grant'. . . . At the next, another exclaimed 'Shakespeare.' At the next there was a group of little boys, and out of it came a beautiful voice, deeply poetic, calling 'White Mercedes, have you come for me?'"

It was no white Mercedes (Randall's preferred make of sports car) that came for Lady Bates, not even the Angel of Death. She just slipped away, as unobtrusively as she had lived.

Around the time that Randall Jarrell was composing "Lady Bates" (1948), he was also reading the Breton poet Tristan Corbière,[3] whom he was to translate in Greensboro in the late 1940s with "*Le Poète Contumace.*" Ending in a hermit-poet's tearing up the letter which constitutes the poem and throwing the pieces into the fog, it parallels "Burning the Letters." Four of Corbière's rondels (one, two, three, and six) appear adapted in *The Seven-League Crutches* as the sequence "Afterwards" (the French title of the six by Corbière is *Rondels pour après*.) The name of Jarrell's collection, in fact, coincides with the expression he coined for Corbière's style in his *The Nation* review of an anthology of the French poet's work: "Puns, mocking half-dead metaphors, parodied clichés, antitheses and paradoxes, idioms, exploited on every level, are the seven-league crutches on which the poems bound forward" (*Poetry and the Age*, p. 147). This sentence mirrors Jarrell's own laminated structures, as in his mature lyrics, most pertinent among them "The End of the Rainbow."

Because of the resemblances between "Afterwards" and "Lady
Bates," a pause to consider Corbière is here in order. In some ways, as
in his use of submerged images portraying the psyche, Corbière was
an ancestor of the Surrealists, as Jarrell may be said to be their descen-
dant, an affinity making him, out of all recent American poets, the
closest to the British David Gascoyne, author of a history of Surrealism
and the leading exponent of it abroad, silent as his muse has been since
the 1930s.

During his lifetime only a slim volume of Tristan Corbière's verse
was published (*Les amours jaunes.)* It remained unnoticed until Paul
Verlaine discovered it, and it was revived again by Ezra Pound and T.
S. Eliot. That Pound was instrumental in attracting Jarrell's attention
to Corbière is implied in this excerpt from the appraisal in *The Nation*
of the McElroy translation of the Breton writer: "Pound called Corbière the most touching of poets—the *Rondels pour après* make his
remark seem as truthful as it is unexpected" (*Poetry and the Age*, p.
159). In the same review he quotes the first "Afterwards" rondel in
French, attributing to it "a cruel and magical tenderness" (p. 161).

Like the monologue to Lady Bates, "Afterwards" speaks to a dead
child, whom Geoffrey Brereton, writing of its original, identifies with
the poet Corbière become a child again who lies in his grave and listens
to a visitor above it, the woman he loves;[4] this explication may well
hold since the title of the first rondel is "Posthumous sonnet." Brereton
lauds the rondels as song-poems (Jean d'Udine has set four of the six to
music). He likes them better than the best known of all Corbière selections, "La Rapode foraine e la Pardon de Sainte-Anne," that mixture
of simplicity and compassion which has much in common with "Lady
Bates."

In Jarrell's first rondel, the opening line "Sleep: here's your bed . . .
You'll not come, any more, to ours" corresponds to "Lady Bates'"s
"There is a bed of your own/ Here where a few stones/ Stick up in the
tall grass dried to hay." Few black children, either in the shacks scattered throughout the rural South or in the grim "high risers" of the
industrialized North, had or have beds of their own. In the opening
pages of Richard Wright's novel *Native Son*, little and not-so-little ones
of both sexes share with their mother a rat-infested bedroom in a Chicago slum, the boys having to turn their backs while the girls and their
mother dress. Now that she is dead, Lady Bates need not share, though
her siblings do not envy her, the clay cave in the cemetery for ".The
Colored," one familiar to Jarrell being the Eastern Star cemetery
adjoining the University of the South in Sewanee, Tennessee, a campus

he visited while at Vanderbilt, during vacations at nearby Monteagle with the Taylors, and in 1961 when he lectured there.

The French line rendered by Jarrell as "Your tongue is all grass" is transformed in "Lady Bates" to "Eating the sweet white heart of the grass." Corbière's intimation of the dissolution of the body sends a shiver of fright through the reader: the eater become the eaten; by transference "Lady Bates" in this verse has much the same effect. The child is pictured as eluding the pair of angels sent to fetch her, a fugitive who is lost even from God, hidden away in the Land of Nowhere (the nest of the cuckoo that builds no nest). She is chewing on pieces of succulent wild grass, as most of us did when children.

The musicality and startling images of Corbière come through in the second stanza of "Afterwards":

> Sleep: they'll call you star-snatcher, bareback-rider
> Of the rays! . . . though it will be dark there, very dark.
> And the angel of attics, at dusk—lean spider,
> Hope—comes to spin, for your vacant brow, its webs.

If Brereton is right, Corbière's picture of himself after death, freed from the bonds of space and time, electrifies the first sentence here with an energy not cancelled out by the aftermath of utter darkness. The passage has none of the Jarrellian horror equated with paralysis in the speech Death croons to Lady Bates, a horror achieved also in the wooing of the poet by the moonlight vampire in "Hohensalzburg" and in the beast of "The Child of Courts" before it was transformed, after *Losses*, to "A Hunt in the Black Forest."

In "Lady Bates," as in several of his other lyrics, Randall Jarrell's intense interest in hypnotism becomes part of the meaning. The hypnotist is Death. Guaranteeing the child an awakening in the twilight at the rising of the stars over her grassy grave, he urges: "Try to reach out to one, to the nearest,/ Reach, try to move—/ You can't move, can you?" There is little question that Jarrell was using here the ritual of hypnotism. George Eastbrook suggests that the neophyte in this practice say: "Listen to me. Your eyelids are locked tightly together and you cannot open your eyes, no matter how hard you try."[5] His advice is almost identical with Death's "Try to open your eyes. . . ./ You can't move, can you?/ You're fast asleep, you're fast asleep." Even the movement of this hypnotist's hand is part of the spellbinding, as another authority on the art mentions: "Then say 'Sound asleep.' 'Dead asleep.' 'Down deep asleep.' 'Go deep.' 'Down deep.' And when his

eyes are closed make light passes over the forehead and eyes, touching
them very lightly, but keep on giving the suggestions of deep sleep."[6]
The manual gesture informs Jarrell's "But Death, after the habit of
command,/ Said to you, slowly closing his hand . . ."

The fixed form, rondel, consists usually in fourteen lines arranged in
three stanzas, using two rhymes only, a line from the first serving as
refrain in the others; Jarrell, as required by the change in language,
treats it with freedom, both in prosody and semantics. An example of
the latter is "little thief of starlight" for "enfant, voleur d'étincelles,"
which involves no reference to starlight, only to sparks. The change in
metaphor in Jarrell makes an interesting synonym for Death's macabre
taunting of Lady Bates to "steal the starlight." Only one verse appears
as identical in Corbière's rondel and Jarrell's adaptation: "Il n'est plus
de nuite, il n'est plus de jours," rendered "There're no nights any
longer, there're no days," an idea worded in "Lady Bates" as "There
is no more night, there is no more day," a change in the number of the
two nouns but an avoidance of the awkward contraction.

Dream also links the Corbière quartet, Englished, and "Lady Bates."
The French poet's promise, "Dream: the last fields are all flowers,"
subtly parallels (though it might also be considered a contrast to) Jarrell's merging of the dreamed and the real into a state of nihilism.
Frederick J. Hoffman notes: "One of Jarrell's characteristic themes is
that of the dreamer awakening into a reality either identical with that
of the dream or in some way comparable to it."[7] The speaker in
"Losses" says: "The night I died I dreamed that I was dead." This concept underlies another interweaving: "Afterwards"'s "close your eyes
to see" appears in "Lady Bates" as "If you could open your eyes/ You
would see nothing," taking the Corbière insight a step further. In the
first rondel, to revert to the title of this chapter, *l'ange du plafond*"
emerges as "the angel of attics"; in the second, the angels are introduced as winged Loves, spiritual beings who come after the dead child:
"Oh, the light feet! Love has wings. . . ." But as in "Lady Bates" these
angels fail to reach the object of their search.

The analogy with Randall Jarrell's elegy for Lady is more pronouced
in Rondel 3: "*You're* not afraid of being alone, though—/ Poor little
thing, are you?" with Death's "You're a big girl now, not even afraid/
Of the dark" (earlier "Lady Bates" has emphasized how the child
shares fear with the screech-owl that cries "*Who, who*" through the
dark trees, like the one Mary and Randall used to listen to during their
first years of marriage).

Fantasy is present in both poems, in the way that the wind is personified: in "Afterwards" first as judge, then as policeman ("—*They* drive you out in the cold, those flatfeet!" the last word an Americanism hardly justified by the nineteenth-century *pied-plats*). Nothing could be more opposite than the winged personifications of Aphrodite in the Botticellian *Nascita*, the painting Jarrell used for his "The Birth of Venus," and these figures of authority trying to drive the child out of the grave. Jarrell as fantasist in his apostrophe to Lady Bates presents the wind as a criminal sentenced to a chain gang. Chain gangs in the South were largely composed of black prisoners. The crime for which this wind has been condemned was just an error, after all—its act of blowing the little girl into eternity, like that wind out of a cloud that chilled and killed Poe's Anabelle Lee. Later, Jarrell's wind is promoted to "the governor's kitchen, a trusty for life," an image recollected from those black convicts whom his Nashville uncle Howell Campbell employed as butler, cook, or chauffeur.

The fourth adaptation, with its rushing refrain "Run away, little comet's-hair-comber!," displays the technical tricks of Tristan, as Wallace Fowlie describes these: "A Corbière poem limps and breaks off and recovers when the poet wishes it to express the corresponding sentiment."[8] Randall Jarrell's dartings back and forth among syntactical modes, with repetitions and underlinings and exclamatory phrases, combined with ellipses, conferred an intricacy with which he never finished tinkering, as worksheets testify. He kept trying to make each lyric more and more complicated (in the sense of "folded together"), at the same time preserving that illusion of real talk at which he is unsurpassed, unless it be by Robert Frost, from whom he learned its secret.

Wallace Fowlie's continuation of how Corbière could move from tenderness to a jocular coarseness is exemplified in how, in the first adapted rondel, the kiss under the veil is succeeded by "a smart blow of the censer," which breaks the child's nose. The analogue in "Lady Bates" is the crap game above the grave between the "high-yaller" Angel Day whom the poet rather unexpectedly calls high yellow, and the coal-black angel Night. "Rolling the bones," as playing dice is euphemistically known in the black community, is a frequent method of securing or parting with property: this time the property is Lady Bates's soul. While Randall Jarrell does not specify the winner, he indicates by position that it is the affectionate and sympathetic Night.[9]

Though the small heroine of "Lady Bates" has both a first and a last

name, neither is truly hers. LeRoi Jones made clear to Afro-Americans
and to the world at large this very point when he rejected his "slave
name" for Imamu Baraka. Jarrell's notes call "Lady" a Christian name
(taken at baptism, ordinarily, in honor of a patron saint), but it is more
likely a made-up name, parent-selected; in the beginning probably
self-chosen, similar to many encountered in the South among blacks,
such as Icy Belle, Gentry, Cherry Lee, Wiggins, Ivory, or the more
classical but scarcely Christian Caesar and Ulysses. The delicacy of
"Lady" for the youngster from the wrong side of the railroad tracks,
that part of Greensboro farthest from its aristocracy, gains in connotation by Jarrell's consistent avoidance of "girl," a noun distasteful to
blacks because their grandparents were "boy" and "girl" into their sev-
enties; he is not so delicate with his second protagonist in this pair of
lyrics. In "Lady Bates" only the kind angel Night, of the same hue as
herself, is allowed this privilege with Lady, just as only he can invoke .
the intimacy of "nigger."

Jarrell seldom changes voice within a poem: this one, however, has
a seven-line preamble using the pronoun *she* instead of *you*—a chance
for the poet to talk to himself before he begins to address the dead
child directly:

> The lightning of a summer
> Storm wakes, in her clay cave
> At the end of the weeds, past the mock-orange tree—
> Where she would come barefooted, curled-up-footed
> Over the green, grained, rotting fruit
> To eat blackberries, a scratched handful—
> The little Lady Bates.

She is pictured as having played too long and fallen asleep, waking to
find herself in the middle of an electrical storm in the cavern near the
cemetery, among the graves to which she is accustomed to come in
search of blackberries (possibly a Corbière play on words). The time is
the end of summer, yet some of the fruit is still green, fallen to the
ground like Lady Bates and, like her, destined never to ripen, already
in decay. The willow, often known as the weeping willow, is so dry
that it cannot weep for her, only rustle. The owl, symbol of cruelty and
death in *The Bat-Poet's* "The Bird of Night," is frightened of her, the
ghost intruding on his domain. Whereas Dylan Thomas rejects the role
of elegist in his poem about the child killed in a London air-raid, Jarrell
here offers himself as the single mourner.

The line "Open your eyes, Lady," introduces what resembles "dream work," the term used in psychoanalysis to refer to the process of concealing from the conscious mind the latent content of dreams. "All in all, I think writing a poem in one sense is rather like writing a piece of music and in another sense it is like having a dream," Randall Jarrell is reported to have said.[10] The one-sided "conversation" with Lady Bates is a dream-construct with autobiographical significance, as well as sociological import. Its highly rhymed, strongly accented verse-paragraphs offer glimpses into the underprivileged lives of black children everywhere, not just in the South; their author, marred like Hart Crane by the disadvantages of "sundered parentage," had a right to consider the childhood he experienced and never really grew out of as underprivileged. In view of Jarrell's home situation Frederick J. Hoffman's statement is all but impossible to understand: "It is obvious that Jarrell had had a splendid childhood, though one wonders why it should flood his fancy in the last of his books, close to his death."[11] The conclusion of "90 North," one of the greatest of Jarrell poems, negates Hoffman's view: "Pain comes from the darkness/ And we call it wisdom. It is pain."

Lady Bates's childhood, like Jarrell's, was far from easy but for different reasons. When she was very small (not yet old enough to be plunged in baptism into the river with its red-clay bottom), she had a "real" mother, someone to comfort her back into sleep after terrifying nightmares, someone to "talk away" her fright. But the mother died, and a strict stepmother replaced her, straight out of those fairy tales that brighten with their magic threads the fabric of Jarrell's own poetry as well as shine in refreshed beauty through his translations. Reading "The darning-needles that sew bad girls' mouths shut/ Have sewn up your eyes," one suspects it is this stepmother who scares the child by threatening that if she is unruly the dragonflies ("darning needles") will sew her mouth shut, foreshadowing the "high-yaller" angel's disapproval: "This *bad* young colored lady." "New Georgia," written a little before "Lady Bates," shows a black American soldier dreaming on a captured island in the South Pacific about an even more miserable childhood: "In the days when, supperless, I moaned in sleep/ with the stripes of beating. . . ."

Lady Bates stands enveloped in steam, helping the cross stepmother "Boil clothes in the kettle in the yard," while other children (presumably white) run past the shanty calling "in their soft mocking voices: 'Lady-bug, Lady-bug, fly away home,'" the adverb *home* pregnant in its *double entendre*.

Jarrell picks up the word *home* and uses it in a deeper sense a second time. As in the first Corbière rondel of "Afterwards," Lady Bates is home at last, "resting in the bosom of Jesus" like Sister Caroline of James Weldon Johnson's lyric "Go Down, Death" in *God's Trombones*. Jesus has appeared earlier in Jarrell's poem as a child in that quartet of three:

> When the Lord God and the Holy Ghost and the Child Jesus
> Heard about you, Lady,
> They smiled all over their faces
> And sang like a quartet . . .

The burden of their song is her loss.

The first book publication of "Lady Bates" came in *Losses*; it was reclassified under "Lives" in *Selected Poems*, even though its subject has left life behind. Death is needed to frame a portrait, which without it goes on changing, like Dorian Gray's. M. S. Rosenthal seems to err in his assessment of Jarrell's portrait here as "a humanitarian southerner's attempt to speak to his knowledge of the hurt done to Negroes in a language appropriate to both."[12] If sentimentality be emotion in excess of the cause, it is as hard to fathom why Rosenthal should blame the poem for being sentimental as it is to see why Weisberg finds the death of a black athlete an unlikely subject for an elegy. The accusation in the University of Minnesota pamphlet is harsh: "The worst of Jarrell is concentrated into parts of this poem that mercilessly expose both his condescension and the presumptuousness of his spokesmanship for the girl."[13] This final word, *girl*, is arresting in the light of its connotation as explained above. In the nine lines that he cites as illustrative of Jarrell's defects, Rosenthal misinterprets that "in-group" verbal caress *trifling* ("A black, barefooted, pigtailed, trifling ghost") and misses the humorous intention of "Poor black trash" as a play on "poor white trash," descendants of the carpetbaggers who flourished after the Civil War. As a New Yorker he may not have been aware that inhabitants of the Bible Belt really do refer to a Book of Life in which the Recording Angel enters good and bad deeds ("And it was all written in the Book of Life"). Fundamentalism is as important to a comprehension of this lyric as it is to a Flannery O'Connor short story. Rosenthal, however, becomes more perceptive in its regard when writing of "The Truth," another child-persona poem in which he sees Lady Bates as anguished and bewildered, and like the boy Jarrell, deprived of a unified family.

To objectify his tenderness in "Lady Bates" Jarrell makes use of a double-angel reference: the angelic child in her white baptismal dress and the crap-shooting angel at the tomb whom only the sung question of the "Trinity" identifies as such: "Where are the two we sent to fetch your soul:/ One coal-black, one high-yellow angel?/ Where is night, where is day?" The closing monologue by Death the hypnotist serves a like function. Macabre as is this figure, so often called "the Angel of Death," he at least consoles the child by promising her a waking.

## II  *"A Girl in a Library"*

Except for Peter Taylor (and no one can be sure this exception need be made), Jarrell never had a better friend than Robert Lowell, though their relationship was not free from rivalry. Their exchange of letters, from the Gambier, Ohio, days when they lived as tenants in the house of John Crowe Ransom at Kenyon, right up into the 1960s, can well stand as adequate "Life." In view of how well they understood each other Lowell's choice matters when he singles out the lyric he feels to be the finest in *The Seven-League Crutches:* "My favorite is 'A Girl in a Library,' an apotheosis of the American girl, an immortal character piece, and the poem in which Jarrell best uses his own qualities and his sense of popular culture."[14]

Even granting that Lowell's talent for caricature is here at work, that noun *apotheosis* oversimplifies. During Randall's boyhood, his father and a photographer-partner named Kramer decorated their letterhead for their three studios in California—Hollywood, Long Beach, and San Diego—with a silhouette under which appeared "Portraits for those blessed with the faculty of critical appreciation." The verbal picture "A Girl in a Library" requires this faculty to discern its tone.

Though Jarrell always looked with disapproval at nonacademic college students, his final verdict in the poem goes in favor of this one, or at least of her predecessor in myth. The ways in which she has missed her life trouble him so much that apotheosis does not seem a good appraisal of his theme. He must have taught hundreds such at Greensboro, Urbana, Princeton, Cincinnati, and elsewhere, his kindness reaching out to diligent and frivolous alike, a virtue remembered gratefully by each. When one of these students came to him with a book of his for autographing, he would write into its end-pages any lyric of her choice: Jean Moore, currently on the English faculty of Belmont Abbey in North Carolina, recalls how in her case he did not hesitate even at the long "Deutsch durch Freud." In "A Girl in a

Library" kindness, though intimidated by reproach, conquers, just as it did in his teaching years.

Like Lady Bates, this girl is motionless, though her condition is only temporary, brought on by drowsiness; not yet asleep in the enclave of books, she is well on the way, as the term *object* reveals. She wears no shoes though not for lack of them, Lady Bates's reason. She is nineteen years old, years which "look alike already," as at twenty-nine her twenty-nine will and at forty-nine the forty-nine, unless she dies before the last figure, as the lyric prophesies. Jarrell notices how athletic she is, the "calves muscular with certainties," as they will continue to be when after college she becomes eligible for the tennis and golf clubs of the community. Yet to the character from Pushkin's *Eugene Onegin*, whom Jarrell introduces to comment on her, she is not muscular but merely fat:

> Meanwhile Tatyana
> Larina (gray eyes nickel with the moonlight
> That falls through the willows onto Lensky's tomb;
> Now young and shy, now old and cold and sure)
> Asks, smiling: "But what is she dreaming of, fat thing?"

Though the comparison of this girl's nose to strawberries suggests a pinkish complexion, she has been tanned by the Southern sun; she has "light-brown limbs," like Salome as Jarrell imagines the New Testament beauty who danced away the Baptizer's head at her stepfather's birthday party. The metaphor for her nose ("Three medium-sized pink strawberries") is only one of the several images that equate the girl drifting to sleep in the library with less-than-human life. Soon, out in the corridor or going down the stairs, she will utter sounds meant as language but really those of an animal, "half-squeal, half-shriek," an amusing reflection of a professor's daily encounters with the screamed drawl capable of interpretation only by its peer group; by murdering the parent tongue this noise reenacts the crime of Oedipus. Her brown eyes are those of a calf, her brow low, her arms and legs resembling an apple dumpling dusted with cinnamon. A trapped animal, she is unable to gnaw off one of her legs and get free because, unlike the woman at the Washington Zoo, she does not even realize she is trapped. A dolphin can jump out of the sea that is its prison, but since she is not awake she is powerless to do so. If someone came into the library and asked what she was doing, she would rouse herself, frown like an orangutan, and answer, "I'm studying." At the opening of her blurred eyes the speaker, quite likely her English teacher, sees in them the "uneasy half-soul" of the dog in Kipling's poem, who begs his master to complete the job and give him full humanity.

Though the Bible is on the shelves, along with Pushkin, Sophocles, Kipling, what is Paul's heroically difficult, heroically courageous life to her? In that allusive technique which makes "A Girl in a Library" typical, Jarrell here parodies the apostle's second letter to the Corinthians: "imperiled in the city, in the desert, at sea, by false brothers; enduring labor, hardship, many sleepless nights; in hunger and thirst and frequent fasting, in cold and nakedness" metamorphoses into "in the glass, in one's own eyes,/ In rooms alone, in galleries [the title used for the 'Ludovisi Throne' lyric], in libraries,/ In tears, in searchings of the heart, in staggering joys." As in "Lady Bates," down underneath the surface of this catalog it is of himself that Randall Jarrell writes. This point is underscored by the final stress-shift from iambic demanded by the prose sense: ". . . in one's own eyes."[15]

Remembering how "In my Father's house there are many mansions," the poet defends the girl against Tatyana Larina, not some character chosen at random from all those peopling his interior landscape, crowded from a lifelong passion for reading. What Goethe is to Germany, Pushkin is to Russia. *Eugene Onegin*, with its over four hundred stanzas, is his most renowned work; he himself called it a "free novel," though it might also be called a "free poem" in the tradition of Romanticism. Its pages have attracted famous translators, such as Babette Deutsch and Vladimir Nabokov, whose "Problems of Translating *Onegin* in English"[16] was probably known to Jarrell as former poetry critic for the *Partisan Review* (in which it appeared). A translator closer to home was Walter Arendt, who taught classics and modern languages at Guilford College in Greensboro till 1956, his *Eugene Onegin* winning the Bollingen Award; he also turned into English Rilke, Heine, and *Faust*. Even apart from the fact that both were enthusiasts of Russian literature, his pursuit of a doctorate at the University of North Carolina where Jarrell taught would have brought the two together.

Arendt's lines from Book Three of *Onegin* sum up Jarrell's reason for choosing the whole-hearted Tatyana as a foil for this "uncommitted" girl in the library, meant to taste neither the heights of ecstasy nor the depths of sorrow: "Tatyana loves in good earnest/ And gives herself over unreservedly/ To love, like a dear young child."[17] The alarm (autobiographical) in the face of transience expressed in "A Girl in a Library" occurs in Arendt ten pages on, in Pushkin's self-questioning, born of a sense of loss: "Can it be that frankly and in actual fact,/ Without elegiac conceits/ The springtime of my days has flashed by?"

It is still spring for the girl in the library, though even the Greensboro spring in its most profound loveliness will remain for her a blind date that has stood her up. In the dialogue that Randall Jarrell and Tatyana carry on across her inert form, the poet denies her a capability for dream but also declares her spared the pain that comes when like Rip Van Winkle each of us realizes, if we are reflective at all, how life itself is a dream. Waking or sleeping, the girl knows only instinctual existence: "She purrs or laps or runs, all in her sleep." At most, she is "a kind, furred animal/ That speaks, in the Wild of things, delighting riddles." Finally, still addressing Tatyana Larina, Jarrell likens the student to a chicken, squawking at unexpected death like the chicken in that horrifying episode that he witnessed in childhood as recorded in "The Lost World," when his grandmother twisted the head off a hen, the body jumping out of her hands "To run/ Away from Something/ In great flopping circles," a nightmare never to leave the memory of the boy-spectator, who found in it a cause for dread of death.[18]

The girl in the library argues with the Angel of Death in the platitudes she has been taught in school, slogans about "Facing Reality" and "Meeting Challenges," the capitals signals for Jarrellian irony. She will truthfully protest: "But I'm a *good* girl," the goodness having been prepared for in an earlier phrase, "pure heart." This whole passage projecting her into eternity resembles what the writer-as-novelist says of Miss Batterson in *Pictures from an Institution*: "When she died, the Recording Angel would look at her accusingly, and she would say defensively, 'I haven't done anything,' and he would close his book and sigh—she had not understood at all," any more than Prufrock's cocktail-party companion. But the fate of the girl with her "last firm strange/Uncomprehending smile "remains as ambiguous as that of the heroine in his single novel. Miss Batterson does die toward its end, in a passage that recalls the mythic conclusion to "A Girl in a Library": "Yet perhaps the Recording Angel would reach out to Miss Batterson and touch her with the tip of his finger, and the poor dew would at last thaw, the seed in the tomb begin to sprout"—the seed in the ritual of the Corn King, celebrant of Resurrection. Lady Bates too is promised a resurrection after the day she sleeps through is over.

Besides this novel—a mosaic of Sarah Lawrence and other campuses, exaggerated by wit—Randall Jarrell's *A Sad Heart at the Supermarket* elaborates on this portrait of the nonintellectual student. After an alarming talk during a Christmas-carol party with a girl completely ignorant of Charlemagne, the writer speaks to her teacher, trying to soften his adverse reaction by remarking that the child must be an "exception." The teacher replies: "Exception indeed! She's a nice, normal, well-adjusted girl. She's one of the drum-majorettes and she's Vice-President of the Student Body [again the ironic capitals]; she's had two short stories in the school magazine and she made her own formal [which could hardly have been "pink" and "strapless"] for the informal Sadie Hawkins dance. She's an exceptionally normal girl!" (p. 36) The reader feels that expertise in recipes and basketball rules will come next in a curriculum leading up to the B.S. in Home Economics and the doctorate in Physical Education. The satire, though not without that smile with which Alexander Pope regards the "armaments" of Belinda's dressing table, comes from a sad heart. Friends observed, after his death, on Jarrell's genuine sadness at their failures in taste, which hurt him as cold words would have hurt someone else.

At the outset the poet has said to this girl, "You are very human," despite the later references to the animal and vegetable worlds; and again "O my sister!"—an identification of her with himself in the evolutionary struggle to put on humanity. If it is hardly a compliment to call her "good enough" for this world, the sting is taken away by that trademark of his, the expression "And yet—."

Which of the two girls has the better record in the Book of Life? Is it the more apparently fortunate one on whose waist "the spirit breaks its arm" but who receives as benediction that perfect chiasmus "I love you—and yet—and yet—I love you"? Or is it the child "Held down in the river till she choked," one Sunday evening, as a baptismal candidate wearing "a white dress like an angel's"? The college student who begins to dream only on the Commencement Day of her death, or Lady Bates, who did not live long enough to work as a maid in the homes of the rich or to have her kinky black hair treated till it was as straight as the brown braids and bangs of the girl in the library?

When he died in the fall of 1965, Randall Jarrell had almost completed arranging lyrics for his next book, to be called *Let's See*. In the volume of memorial tributes Robert Phelps says of him: "He simply saw what he saw with the serene, fierce, unflinching disinterest of a recording angel" (p. 138). These two portraits let us, too, "see."

### CHAPTER 4

# Jarrell the Analogist: Poems on Art

IN addition to excelling in such monologues as "Lady Bates" and "A Girl in a Library," Jarrell was one of "the new masters" in re-creating works of art. To understand how this man, who met "death at an early age," preserved the past for the future while at the same time transforming it, one must study at some depth his major lyrics on paintings and statues. One of his greatest gifts was the way "he turned his knowledge—in painting, music, and German, as well as in English literature—to use in poems that give new freshness to the idea of a life of the mind."[1] Though *Who's Who* (1963) lists music as the first of Jarrell's leisure interests, this chapter will deal only with painting, and with sculpture, an art for which "The Clock in the Tower of the Church" and "Man in Majesty," two lyrics not considered here, show that he had a rare feeling.

I    *"The Bronze David of Donatello"*

Painters are often praised for lyricism; a sculptor seldom is. Yet Donatello's commentators have detected an affinity between his David and poetry, the subject itself found in the cadenced prose of Scripture. Art historian H. W. Janson notes the resemblance in his phrase "the calm lyricism of the David."[2] The Florentine sculptor possesses in common with Jarrell a developing vision of man against the monstrous background of natural forces, threatened but unvanquished even in death.

The poem in question begins with a verbal description as stylized as its source: "A sword in his right hand, a stone in his left hand,/ He is naked. Shod and naked. Hatted and naked." Already one senses something unnatural about this "hero." That he occupied Jarrell's thoughts is clear from the fact that a large framed detail of this Donatello hung above the dresser in his bedroom at Greensboro, with other photographs he cherished. Robert Lowell remarks in the memorial volume, edited with Robert Penn Warren and Peter Taylor, how among "the

bright, petty, pretty sacred objects he accumulated for his joy and sol-
ace" there were reproductions of this sculpture, the most significant of
the adjectives perhaps the second one, *petty*.[3]

Jarrell despised cocktail parties, with their Prufrockian small talk,
and worse, gossip; he preferred a quiet existence in the "little house in
the wood," the first piece of real estate he ever owned. Here, in the
then "wilderness" of Greensboro's outskirts, he could put down roots
himself as he planted the trees which, grown tall, make the property
so beautiful today. Donatello, likewise, felt the need for contemplation,
retreating from Florence, with its hedonistic de Medici court, to the
more mystical town of Siena, later renowned for its saints, like Cath-
erine and Bernardine. Though to a lesser degree than Chekhov and
Rilke, Donatello was a "second self" for Jarrell, who could comtem-
plate for hours the Pacific at Laguna Beach and the truths it evoked
for him. To put the alter ego concept another way, one might note that
Donatello served Jarrell, indirectly, in the sense that Bertran de Born
and François Villon did Pound, as a persona. To either might apply
this sentence meant for Donatello: "A sense of desolation and inward-
ness pervades these works of the aging master, now alone in an alien
world,"[4] a "lost" world which for Jarrell, as he passed the mid-century
mark, came to take on possibilities of exploration as a world more truly
"found" than the one Columbus discovered.

Jarrell went to Europe for the first time in the summer of 1948,
when he lectured on American poetry at Salzburg, a session well
recorded in lyric after lyric. His second trip was made with Mary von
Schrader Jarrell, herself a seasoned visitor to Florence, where the
Museo Nazionale has been the home of Donatello's David since the
1880s. One can imagine the young couple exclaiming at its lifelikeness,
like the poet David McCann: "At the warm stone of his/ flesh he made
the whole city kneel!"[5] Later, they probably both viewed another representation (this one in marble) of the shepherd who killed Goliath,
kept in Washington's National Gallery: a clothed, reflective lad with
his foot placed gently on the giant's head, which resembles in its nobil-
ity that of the heroic *The Dying Gaul*.[6]

Sylvia Plath composed one of her longest poems (now available only
in a rare book library) on a Paul Klee Medusa for a series projected by
*Art News;* readers of Jarrell have more reason to be grateful to its
editors since an October 1957 issue announces Randall Jarrell as the
inaugurator in that number of a fascinating sequence of art reproductions juxtaposed to poetic treatment of them. Seven halftones accom-

pany Jarrell's lyric on David's triumph over Goliath, hinting at the
meditations "in the round" that must have been the genesis of detail
after detail in his rendering of what the masterpiece said to him. Just
opposite Jarrell's first stanza is an unusual facial view of the shepherd,
showing how "The mouth's cut Cupid's bow, the chin's unwinning
dimple/ Are tightened, a little oily." Near it is a full-length back study
disclosing one single heavy tassel and ribbon; in the poem "The ribbons
of his leaf-wreathed, bronze-brimmed bonnet/ Are tasseled," the locks
of hair lying in separation both in the bronze and in the lyric. David's
genitals as "this green/ Fruit now forever green" match the green
navel oranges of "Lady Bates," neither fruit nor child ever to ripen.
The bottom photograph center, in *Art News*, shows Goliath's eyes not
open as they would have been in reality after the sudden death, but
closed in dream, a dream untouched by the bloody severance which
had occasioned it.

Repetitive designs in the verses echo those in the sculpture: the *a b
a b* of the first line as quoted, the host of identical rhymes (*naked,
somehow, dances, face, triumph* are employed as symmetrically as the
formal leaves and fringe embossed on the greaves surprisingly worn by
the shepherd-champion of the Israelites).

Suzanne Ferguson's *The Poetry of Randall Jarrell* devotes four
insightful pages to "The Bronze David of Donatello,"[7] which lyric Jarrell himself felt had enough weight to conclude his 1960 National-
Book-Award winner, *The Woman at the Washington Zoo*. She bases
some of her comments on the wealth of worksheets now in the special
Jarrell collection, at the University of North Carolina (Greensboro)
Library—pages which reveal the metamorphic struggle toward final
form. The ambiguities remain unanswered, both in Donatello's metal
medium and Jarrell's verbal one, except for the clear conviction shining through either that beyond the courage of David rises compassion,
a greater virtue. Both artists emphasize the horror that can be present
in victory and the beauty in defeat. Elsewhere Donatello was to cap-
ture the same enigma in his rendition of a beheading from another
scriptural source, that of Holofernes by Judith. Janson, cited above in
respect to the lyrical quality of Donatello's portrayal of David, compares the David to Salome, in a New Testament decapitation, calling
the lad "le beau garçon sans merci."[8]

Donatello's David was the first "detached nude" in Western art since
the classical period. This nakedness, mentioned three times by Jarrell
at the outset and stressed throughout, seems an affront. In the natural-
istic poem, the sensuous adolescent torso ("the whore Medusa's" face)

has petrified into death a creature worthy of a finer exit from the drama of God's dealings with His chosen people. What wings are depicted belong to Goliath, not David, and in the bronze they grow out of the giant's body in contrast to the possibility of their being armorial decorations. Jarrell follows the sculptor here:

> . . . The head's other wing (the head is bearded
> And winged and helmeted and bodiless)
> Grows like a swan's wing up inside the leg;
> Clothes, as the suit of a swan-maiden clothes,
> The leg.

All the delicacy of Jarrell's swan-references based on ballet surfaces in these lines, which continue to extend the metaphor until Goliath is unmistakably identified with the magical Swan Maiden, in Jarrell (as in Yeats's tribute to Lady Gregory) a figure of immortality. The slain giant lying in the dust beneath the callow destroyer has entered into an eternal glory, a new light falling from heaven upon his face. In Donatello this sweet success of the vanquished is brought out by Janson in an analysis of the *putti* engraved on the visor of Goliath's helmet.[9] To achieve this effect, Jarrell creates his own beatitude, close in spirit to the Sermon on the Mount and the Canticle of the Sun: "Blessed are those brought low,/ Blessed is defeat, sleep blessed, blessed death." That the "beatitude" is a sort of autobiographical wish-fulfillment is the reading given it by Peter Davison in an essay significantly entitled "Self-Revelation in the New Poetry": of Jarrell he says: "Why do the poems about art and literature seem to have more wholeness than those about human beings? And even in these, as in the fascinating long poem about the *David* of Donatello, fatigue conquers in the end."[10] This coda corresponds also to Whitman's carol that Jarrell so much admired in "Out of the Cradle Endlessly Rocking ," that hymn to the dark mother, always gliding near.

## II   *"The Birth of Venus"*

As provocative to thought as the expression of this "angelic" victor gazing unmoved at his first corpse is the Aphrodite of Botticelli's most famous canvas, also in Florence, the *Nascita di Venere*, or *The Birth of Venus*. This painting is a version of the Anadyomene tradition begun by the lost work of the ancient Apelles.

Written in 1952 but still unpublished at the time of Jarrell's death, anthologies since have made "The Birth of Venus" one of the better-known examples of his poetry. Linked as loosely to Botticelli as the latter was to Donatello, whose David he once incorporated into a painting of Lucretia's death, the poem is as much an invitation to a robust kind of sensuality as the painting is a challenge to any such defilement. Botticelli's rosy cloak, held out by an Ovidian figure—a modest, substantial garment molded as if in statuary— becomes in Jarrell a seductive, transparent veil cast over Venus by a rained-out cloud: "Having rained itself out,/ The cloud throws over her a transparent veil," blurring the impression of divinity so well expressed by Randall Jarrell in the preceding sentence:

> In the light of the setting sun
> Her body is incandescent with rainbows
> Of mother-of-pearl.

After the just-over storm which has washed away the slime from the voluptuous nude's flesh, her eyes still dazzled from the brilliant tropical fish in the coral forests of the sea ("Disguised as flowers of paradise"), Venus glows in the divine splendor she enjoyed as queen of her brother Neptune's kingdom under the waves. But not for long.

Botticelli's art, the apex of Neoplatonism in his day, is often referred to as poetry in that he was more interested in the ideas to be depicted than in the images; he felt painting to be the vehicle of knowledge, a role which the Romantics accorded to poetry. Thus it was natural for his de Medici patron to set him to work collaborating with the popular Renaissance poet Angelo Poliziano, illustrating for the villa outside Florence Poliziano's *La Giostra*. From this villa the Aphrodite rising from the sea was moved to Florence's Uffizi gallery where Jarrell studied it in detail before rejecting its central theme.

If what Donatello and Jarrell did to the heroic David, ancestor of the Messiah and extolled by Hebraic tradition, was a turnabout, even more so is this caricature of Botticelli's wistful dreamer on her cockle-shell, blown on by personified winds amid a rain of immortal blossoms, edged with gold from the Botticellian brushes. For Ezra Pound, this dreamer on her shell, still a part of the divine changelessness of Paradise, is an organizing principle in *The Cantos,* a gold thread through their labyrinth. His use of the goddess has nothing in common with Jarrell's sex symbol netted in sandy seaweed, with tiny crabs scurrying down her limbs. The "shameful birth"—her origin from the sea-foam gathered around Uranus' genitals after Cronos had castrated him—is a tag end out of Hesoid which has no place in the lustrous fabric of Botticelli's apostrophe to Love. In Jarrell whatever witnesses there were to Aphrodite's shame have been tumbled to their death by the thunderbolt which has knocked them out of their fishermen's huts into the tongueless sea. The whole rather comic representation links itself to the grotesquerie of Donatello's (and Jarrell's) tasseled hat and military boots of David, in contrast to the then-revolutionary stark nakedness of the rest of his body.

Botticelli's inscrutable and aloof deity blown upon by flower-embroidered winds is awaited by an elegantly clothed companion of her own sex, not by a traveling salesman, as in Jarrell. Yet even Botticelli may have had some universal concept in mind other than what would have occurred to Ficino or other Neoplatonists of his century. Gabriele Mandel has identified the Quattrocento artist's Venus with *Humanitas:* "Humanity is born to civilization and coming out of nowhere lands on the shores of nature, who welcomes and clothes it."[11] No abstract noun in the corpus of Jarrell's poetry is more prominent that the generic *man*. In accord with his use of feminine masks for his masculine protagonists, Venus may well stand for life from the sea becoming, at last, the life of Man.

### III   *"The Knight, Death, and the Devil"*

Three years after his initiation of the poem/painting parallels for *Art News* with the Donatello, Randall Jarrell contributed a forty-line verbal re-creation of Albrecht Dürer's 1514 etching *The Knight, Death, and the Devil*. How important this work was to him can be judged by the double-page photographic spread placed in the center of the memorial volume by his friends, and showing him holding a book with a large detail of the Knight and a page of commentary opposite, the date line beneath the photograph reading June 1957. Derived from Erasmus's *Handbook of the Christian Soldier*, this engraving, like Donatello's David and Venus Anadyomene considered as Humanity, can stand for man's progress through life as Pilgrim. One is reminded, in a strange correspondence, of the verses carved on the Sligo tombstone of that literary hero, William Butler Yeats, whose photograph Jarrell kept near him: "Cast a cold eye/ On Life, on Death,/ Horseman, pass by." In the Bösch-like forest of the allegory the mysterious rider ("Horseman") proceeds unfrightened by the illusory antagonists depicted by Dürer as trying to impede his progress.[12]

The engraving resembles a stage setting, of no depth, though a few attempts at perspective appear in the Knight's foreshortened foot in its stirrup and in the diminished size of the distant castles possibly meant to stand for Virtue, or for the Heavenly Jerusalem. As Jarrell transforms the Dürer symbolism ("His castle—some man's castle, set on every crag"), he emphasizes the uniqueness of each human being's aspiration. The Knight derives in part from Revelation 19:11: "And I saw heaven opened, and behold a white horse; and he that sat upon him was called Faithful and True, and in righteousness he doth judge and make war." Greensboro student Barbara Lovell's poem "Losses," quoted from in the final chapter, includes this line: "I have not become that knight of Dürer's/ You admired," an indication of how Jarrell interwove his life in the classroom with this "spectator sport" of Dürer-watching. His calling the Knight's horse "dun" is one more touch of the everyday.

No adequate attempt can here be made to trace the development of Jarrell strategies from "The Rage for the Lost Penny" in John Ciardi's *Five Young American Poets* of 1940, to "The Knight, Death, and the Devil" of the 1950s; yet it is evident that the poet's evolution from the neo-Augustan forms of his Vanderbilt friends the Fugitives was quite far along by the time the poem appeared. Analogously, Dürer's method underwent transformation from the *Self-Portrait* done at thirteen (he was always magnetized by his own reflected countenance, as was Jarrell, who could never pass a mirror without looking into it) to the three *Meisterstiche* of 1513–14, among which is *The Knight, Death, and the Devil*. (*Saint Jerome in His Study*—the subject of another Jarrell poem—and *Melencolia I* are the other two of these famous if puzzling artifacts.)

It seems important in these pages to scrutinize the minutiae of the Dürer because that is just what Randall Jarrell did, hour after hour, with his magnifying glass, and not only the *Art News* engraving but others as well. After Albrecht Dürer's trip to Venice (a crucial event in his life) he dwelt mainly on the Apocalypse with its recurrent horse symbols and plethora of angels, those spiritual beings employed by Jarrell in over thirty of his lyrics, and always in the Christian tradition rather than in the Mohammedan style affected by Rilke in the *Duino Elegies*. Influenced by the painter Matthew Grünewald, Dürer's *Four Horsemen of the Apocalypse* has a skeletal rider with the same "shock-headed, cornshuck-bearded" look as Jarrell's Death. The latter imaged as a scarecrow figure in "A Country Life" ("A bird that I don't know/ Hunched on his light-pole like a scarecrow") calls out a *memento mori* to the human observer of the farm scene. Death's mount in Dürer's *Four Horsemen of the Apocalypse* is galloping instead of grazing on herbs, and is rope-bridled as in Jarrell's poem though the other three mounts have leather reins. *Soldier on Horseback*, another Dürer now in Vienna, coincides with Jarrell's lines in several respects:

> In fluted mail; upon his lance the bush
> Of that old fox [the Devil]; . . .

the lance as well as the tail-trophy attached to it bearing witness to victory; and in regard to the rider, " . . . his face is firm / In resolution, in absolute persistence." This horse is stopped, not moving steadfastly on toward journey's end, but the swordhilt clasped calmly in the soldier's right hand anticipates the greater work, with its iconography of the good man's perseverance through the Dark Wood of this life.[13]

Had Dürer etched only the horse, rider, and dog, leaving out the phantasmagoria of the background, the result might have been an artistic success comparable to his *Equestrian Monument of Gattamelata* in Padua, but such an exclusion would have omitted the ethical meaning, that indicated by the smile of all three central figures as they press forward toward the City of God. The sacred history involved begins with the skull, a device then popular in art, e.g., Pesellino's *The Crucifixion with Saint Jerome and Saint Francis*, now in Washington, D.C. This skull derives from the legend that a seed from the Tree of Life was placed in the mouth of the dead Adam and from it sprang the Tree of Jesse, which was destined to bear the Redeemer. It is odd that Jarrell does not include it, in view of Mary Jarrell's anecdote in *The Biography of a Poem: Jerome*, which tells how Randall liked to cover with a finger the skull in *Der Heilige Hieronymus*, take it away, and re-cover, exclaiming "Boy, nothing in art talks like a human skull."[14] The reason for ignoring both skull and salamander of the original may be that Jarrell had a profound sense of how completely the Knight himself ignored these echoes of the Edenic catastrophe.

To unify his compositions, since, like Botticelli, Dürer paid scant attention to perspective, the creator of *The Knight, Death, and the Devil* led the eye from point to point, from the head of Death's horse to the climax: the tip of the rider's lance, signifying conquest. In Jarrell, a series of participles imitates this ascent of diagonals: there are eighteen instances of *-ed* verbal adjectives as well as eleven other participial forms. A typical example of patterning through participles is this excerpt on the bat-winged pikeman, a character out of nightmare: "The pocked, ribbed, soaring crescent of his horn,/ A scapegoat aged into a steer; boar-snouted." By his array of strong accents and of semicolons, the poet calls attention to these segments featuring words stemming from verbs and retaining their dynamism.

It is natural to connect the Dürer-Jarrell confrontation with diabolical forces to the poet's longtime absorption in Faust. Though he has often been accused of bleakness touching on despair, Jarrell's devotion to Dürer picture and Goethe epic refutes the label of hopelessness about the human predicament. This belief in man's capacity to overcome, even when all seems doomed as after the Faustian pact sealed in blood, is a Renaissance characteristic. Well might Jarrell in *A Sad Heart in the Supermarket*, have been thinking of Dürer's *The Knight, Death, and the Devil* when he wrote of Bamberg's *Saint Elizabeth:* "Man's ability to bear and disregard—to look out into, to look out past anything in his world—has been expressed as well in a few other works of art, but never, I think, better; she seems to look out into that Being which has cancelled out the Becoming which the Rider [another Bamberg statue] looks into and is" (p. 183). Even Friedrich Nietzsche, though anti-Christian, saw Dürer's Knight as "a symbol of our existence."[15]

The timelessness of the allegory, how it applies not only to the first death but to each one since, has made it a fitting vehicle for one of the finest elegies commemorating Randall Jarrell, John Wheatcroft's, which contains this passage:

> You are not expecting, I know, pale horse,
> pale rider to come clopping along the concrete,
> damming traffic, and rousing horns,
> or ambling diffidently on the shoulder,
> lingering perhaps to forage clumps of grass
> the highway crew has missed, for champing.[16]

This poem, which transfers the Quattrocento procession to modern North Carolina, builds into elegy one of the "immortal concepts" of Pound which Jarrell found exemplified in Albrecht Dürer.

## IV   *"Jerome"*

So great was Randall Jarrell's predeliction for Dürer that it is natural to find a second lyric devoted to the artist. Mary Jarrell's book-length account of this other poem, "Jerome," deserves the gratitude of readers for the marvelously patient explication of his craftsmanship and enriching biographical data which add so much to Jarrell's modernization of Dürer's glimpse into the holy life of Jerome, saint-translator of the Bible. The section "Reflections on Jerome" tells how, during his Library of Congress consultantship, he checked out for the entire two years the largest volume he could find of Dürer (which he pronounced *Deer-a*), regularly turning its pages as if it were a spiritual calendar. She relates how he loved to show her his favorites under a reading glass, especially the *Apocalypse of Saint John* and *Saint John Devouring the Book*, although this best friend of Jesus among the disciples was never to have a poem centered on him in the Jarrell canon.

The lyric celebrating the virtues of an admired psychiatrist (imagined, actual, or a composite) not only involves several Dürer Jeromes but depictions by El Greco, Titian, Carpaccio, and others. As is true of Saint Lucy, the galleries in Washington, D.C., and elsewhere are full of Saint Jeromes. Some things in "Jerome" deviate from all of the reproductions in Mrs. Jarrell's biography of the poem: the three woodcuts showing the saint (a) curing his lion, (b) in his cell, or (c) in a cave; the 1514 engraving of him in his study, and a medallion done a year or so later. The foreword states that "no single Dürer quite met the needs of Jerome's dream [that part of the poem which is a flashback to Renaissance religious art] so that, in the way dreams gather materials from life, material from several Dürers was gathered for this dream" (p. 15).

The psychiatrist dreamer here is meant as a complement to the woman at the Washington Zoo, on the authority of the poet himself, but it can also be seen as a complement to the Dürer Knight. Some art critics have viewed the two engravings as a pair, meant to be contemplated in relation to one another. The doctor in question has handled his own alienation, coming out of self-treatment a healed healer instead of a victim of life like the woman government worker who finds herself on the verge of despair as she wanders alone amidst the cages of animals in the Rock Creek Park Zoo. When Jarrell began the poem, his chief interest (according to the facsimile worksheets) lay in the psychiatrist's patients, called the "fools" in the first title he gave this lyric. The only analyst to whom the psychiatrist himself comes for consultation is that silent listener Night, to whom he tells his dreams over and over, in a monologue during which toads become dragons, a transformation appearing initially and never abandoned throughout all the versions. This change is the opposite of what an analysand would hope for, during his waking hours, if he went to a psychiatrist for therapy.

Randall Jarrell, who knew Freud's writings intimately from repeated readings, was at least as much at home in the subconscious as the conscious, as perusal of both *The Complete Poems* and the children's books (composed or translated) will affirm. In "Jerome," once the censor is off duty, ego and id get switched into "Where Ego was there Id shall be." Examining the worksheets in *The Biography of a Poem: Jerome*, one laments the excision of "at the bottom of the night the light/ is darkness," a sentence of Poundian simplicity which here represents the total control of the conscious by the id. As a matter of fact, the history of the poem involves a scattering of such beautiful discards, though none but the maker has the right to feel any of them indispensable to the theme.

This psychiatrist knows well the validity of Yeats's refrain in "The Stolen Child" on how *the world's more full of weeping/ Than we can understand.*" Jarrell, who loved Yeats, probably had the Sligo faeries' song in mind when he devised this other discard: "and all the world/ lies weeping." In compassion ("suffering with") the doctor listens all day, trying to help the sufferers to understand so that normal joy may replace weeping, but when his office hours and domestic chores are finished and he is free to sleep, he confides to the dragon Night the following dream, a mosaic of Dürers:

> *... I see*
> *– There is an old man, naked, in a desert, by a cliff.*
> *He has set out his books, his hat, his ink, his shears*
> *Among scorpions, toads, the wild beasts of the desert.*
> *I lie beside him—I am a lion.*
> *He kneels listening. He holds in his left hand*
>
> *The stone with which he beats his breast, and holds*
> *In his right hand, the pen with which he puts*
> *Into his book, the words of the angel:*

The old man is listening to the Spirit of the Lord as he translates the Scriptures, invoking it through the small crucifix which is present in each of the Dürers reproduced in Mary Jarrell's book. No angel appears in any: Christ is the "Angel" of whom the saint asks counsel, "The angel up into whose face he looks."

Among the various Dürer depictions, the one most nearly identical to the psychiatrist's dream is *Saint Jerome in Penitence*. Here the hermit, called "naked" in the poem, is so at least from the waist up, and situated in a desert landscape which ends in a cliff. The next two lines—the setting out of his scholarly materials—would require an interior like that in the *Study* engraving, were it not for the "scorpions, toads, the wild beasts of the desert." The dreaming doctor, changed into the companion lion, lies quietly beside the kneeling, reverent penitent intent upon his task of transcribing the Word. Originally in the manuscripts the dragon Night was reduced to a lizard coiled on the anachronistic red hat (Jerome was not a cardinal, but the tradition was so strong that Cardinal Albrecht of Brandenburg had the painter Louis Cranach execute his portrait as Saint Jerome).

The only lion in the Renaissance dream, contrary to the ubiquitous leonine presence in the Dürers, is the doctor himself, at least at night, in his bare apartment resembling a cell. But waiting for him at the Zoo, which he approaches in happiness, unlike his feminine double (miserable as she sees in every animal-enclosure beings more fortunate than her own trapped self) is his friend the lion, to whom he has brought a lump of liver, which he stops at the grocer's to buy. He too, like the woman, is a civil servant, but in his case the adjective means courteous; in hers, governmental. Jarrell's empathy for the office worker is heightened by his making her the colorless negative of the cheerful human being who walks toward his lion "under leaves, in light," ready to begin another day's ministrations. The dragon Night in "Jerome" wrestles with the world "And after a long time changes it." The woman at the Washington Zoo in her apostrophe to the vulture, be he man as Perseus-deliverer or Death itself, can only scream out, silently, the unanswered prayer: "Change me!"

V   *"The Old and the New Masters"*

The most comprehensive pictorial analogy in Jarrell is "The Old and the New Masters," first collected in *The Lost World*, 1965. In its over sixty lines it unites important works by Pieter Brueghel the Elder, Georges de la Tour, Hugo Van der Goes, Paolo Veronese, as well as incorporating Abstract-Expressionism techniques. The poem begins with Brueghel's *Landscape with the Fall of Icarus* so that Randall Jarrell may make his own contribution to that seminar on pain as felt or not felt by the uninvolved: those cast in the role of spectators or not noticing at all. In the parable of the Good Samaritan, Jesus showed a spectrum of attitudes toward the suffering of others. W. H. Auden reduces the possibilities to a single view in "Musée des Beaux Art"; it is with a variant of his famous first line, "About suffering they were never wrong, the Old Masters," that Jarrell opens "The Old and the New Masters." By so doing, he entered into this seminar wherein E. E. Cummings, William Carlos Williams, and other poets have been participants. John Lucas in a privately printed lyric consisting of only three words—"sometimes/ somebody/ cares"—restores the mystery of free will lost for rhetorical purposes in Auden; Jarrell, on a more extended scale, does the same.

The author of "The Old and the New Masters" never tired of Brueghel, any more than of Dürer. He took advantage of every opportunity to see the originals in Europe and elsewhere, and he spent much time leafing through his German "Brueghel book," a 1941 volume introduced by Max Dvorak. He loved its *Landschaft mit dem Sturz des Icarus*, the impetus for Auden's poem. A shepherd stares at the sky, a farmer on the earth, whereas only a single sheep looks at the tragically falling boy. The one human being visible in the "splendid ship" is unaware of the drowning.

When Jarrell was in his twenties and recalling the conclusion of an unhappy love affair, he addressed himself to the problem of the sharing of pain in "A Summer Night," more inspired by the insight (oversimplification though it be) of Auden than by a criticism of that insight. The autobiographical protagonist lies, in memory, near a weeping girl on the sands of a beach. He feels guilty about his inability to respond to her love:

> ... The overmastering
> Tears roll over it [her face]. I shut my eyes.
> So you wept, I cared; still ...
> 　　　　The absurd eyes
> That watch the stranger crying in their midst—
>
> Not amused, not pitying, that merely watch—
> The eyes of man. ...

Though this lyric was written in the 1930s, it ends with the same two words, "I see," which preface the psychiatrist's dream in "Jerome," words illustrative of how, even as early as this juvenilia, Jarrell hurt when others hurt, even though he adds to the above lines Auden's condemnation of man as indifferent.

Introducing his mature meditation, "The Old and the New Masters," he counters W. H. Auden's half-truth with "About suffering, about adoration, the old masters/ Disagree," as of course they do, changing beliefs as reflected in art being largely responsible (the Renaissance, a period of deep faith, embraced the other end of Auden's emotional detachment). Whereas "Musée des Beaux Arts" declares that suffering "takes place/ While someone else is eating or opening a window or just walking dully along," Jarrell in his opening stanza denies that such apathy exists; rather, "When someone suffers, no one else eats/ Or walks or opens the window." This statement is no more designed to be universal than Auden's; in fact, neither Renaissance art nor life bears it out. Brueghel's canvas of Christ carrying his cross— that welter of humanity dwarfing the struggle of the Redeemer by its humdrum activities swirling across the painting surface—negates the poet's "no one breathes/ As the sufferers watch the sufferer." But in the second painting treated, Georges de La Tour's *Saint Sebastian Mourned by Saint Irene*, the instance of compassionated suffering Jarrell has chosen, his denial of Auden has justification.

In *Art News* (Summer, 1956) Randall Jarrell had fully discussed the excellences of the de La Tour painting in his article remonstrating against Abstract-Expressionism, to which the editor appended the unauthorized-by-author title "The Age of the Chimpanzee." He presents *Saint Sebastian Mourned by Saint Irene* as a metaphor of the world wherein the work exists: a geometry of scaled relationships polyphonic, as against the "man-less," "Nature-less" art following after (but falling far short of) Jackson Pollock. The concealed light typical of de La Tour appears in this lyric as "The flame of one torch is the only light": this indirect illumination is the painter's trademark (cf. *Magdalen with the Night Light* in the Louvre, or *The Education of the Virgin* in New York's Frick Museum).[17]

In the next line, "All the eyes" means three pairs: Irene's; the red-gowned torch-holder's; a hooded friar's, of whose face the artist has painted merely a crescent against the wall of dark shadows, above the man's interlaced hands bathed in fireglow. This last-named figure stands for Franciscanism, a spirituality which became more and more dominant in de La Tour. As is common in art history, Jarrell confuses monastic with mendicant orders: "Beside her a *monk's* hooded head is bowed" (italics mine). The fourth person, a maid servant weeping into a white cloth, is a clear refutation of the unconcern Auden was to enunciate in the twentieth century. All the mourners seem to be lamenting not the wounded saint but the crucified Jesus:[18] "It is as if they were still looking at the lance,/ Piercing the side of Christ nailed on his cross."

In actuality, Sebastian was not dead in this representation of his arrow-punctured, almost nude body at the feet of the early Christians. A converted nobleman in the army of Diocletian, he had been ordered shot with arrows because of what was regarded as disloyalty to the Empire, his new faith. Left for dead, he was nursed back to health by a wealthy lady of Rome, Irene. Later, the Emperor had him beaten to death by clubs, a martyrdom anticipated in the arrow episode which appealed not only to de La Tour but to Polliuolo, Mantegna, Botticelli. Jarrell must have been familiar, from his two years of Library of Congress service, with the Botticelli depiction, which hangs in the National Gallery in Washington.

Flannery O'Connor alone, among American writers of our century, places at the core of her stories the Passion-Resurrection (inseparable) lived through by each character en route to salvation and climaxed in an unfailing epiphany, often close to the moment of death. In "Everything that Rises Must Converge," this instant of enlightenment occurs to a young man named Sebastian, after de La Tour's saint. Jarrell's account of the centrality of Christ in the Portinari altarpiece painting condenses her view, which is the same as that informing most Renaissance art: empathy.

In the five lines concluding Jarrell's blank-verse commentary on the mourning of Saint Sebastian, the three women and their male companion become other Christs as they stand above the wounded young convert from paganism:

> The same nails pierce all their hands and feet, the same
> Thin blood, mixed with water, trickles from their sides.
> The taste of vinegar is on every tongue
> That gasps, "My God, my God, why hast Thou forsaken me?"
> They watch, they are, the one thing in the world.

Nailed to the cross (time being erased to return them to Golgotha), their hearts rent by the centurion, the taste of the vinegar-soaked sponge in their mouths, the Fifth Word on their lips, they appear to summarize Creation in the arrested flux of "It is consummated."

Picking up the phrase, "the one thing in the world," Jarrell in his poem moves into a verse-parallel of an even greater painting on the same vision, Van der Goes' Nativity altarpiece. With Christ as focal point of the universe, it demonstrates all that "The Age of the Chimpanzee" attributes to painting before the cult of the abstract took over: it is a large work (nineteen by eight feet), a complex but completely unified interrelationship of levels of being revolving around the Divine Birth. Jarrell owned a copy of it, a handsome gilded triptych, and frequently pored over it with his magnifying glass. The Flemish master, like his contemporary Albrecht Dürer, rejected perspective in favor of making the size of figures accord with their importance in simultaneously exposed chapters of sacred narrative radiating from the "small, helpless, human center" at Bethlehem.

Hugo Van der Goes, who earlier had executed *The Adoration of the Magi*, chose another group to concentrate on (the shepherds) when asked by the rich Tommaso Portinari to decorate the family chapel attached to San' Egidio, a church in Florence. They are the first merely human actors mentioned by Randall Jarrell: "The shepherds, so big and crude, so plainly adoring . . ."—so completely different from the usual portrayals up to that time.

The first shepherd, clad in brown, kneels on one knee, staff between breast and forearm, hands as reverently clasped as Dürer's *Praying Hands* though not so uptilted. Blondish and bearded, he is smiling, whereas the man next to him is more serious; clad in dark mantle over a red tunic, his curling black hair further individualizing him, he holds out his hands as if to say, "Come to me." The shepherd who stands behind them, hat in one hand and a spade in the other, is open-mouthed in amazement; with his capuche he resembles a friar, perhaps Van der Goes's little tribute to the order which in Umbria in the thirteenth century began the tradition of the Christmas crib. This rustic realism and spontaneous gesture, this introduction of ordinary folk in the peasant garb of their trade, with the shepherd's dog prominently shown, represented an innovation far from the secularization of Veronese, treated later in Jarrell's lyric.

In the Portinari altarpiece, the creatures most in touch with the "miraculous birth" are all done on the same scale: Mary, thumbs and fingers lightly touching as if to form a bouquet, eyes interlocked with those of the tiny Babe ("the Virgin who kneels/ Before her child in worship"); the burly shepherd, their differing emotions expressed as well by hands as countenances; on the other side of Jesus, an elderly Joseph, his sandals off as if in homage to the holiness of the very ground, his clasped hands duplicating those of the oldest shepherd. Describing this center panel, Jarrell does not mention Joseph but is drawn rather to the adoring Mother in her dress of rich royal blue, her thin hair in separated auburn strands, a hollow between the cords of her neck, with no ornaments at all, in defiance of the Flemish custom. Behind her falls a shadow, as of the Cross.

Relegated to the wings is the "medium-sized," kneeling donor, Tommaso Portinari, with his sons, Antonio and Pignello, while on the opposite side is his wife, Maria, with their daughter, Margherita. The bigness of the patron saints, alluded to by Jarrell, symbolizes how their grandeur as citizens of Paradise exceeds the earthly glory of those whom they protect. The canonized quartet consists of Thomas Aquinas, Anthony the Hermit, Margaret, and Magdalen, for whom the family members have been named. Over the head of the donor's wife are "the Magi out in the hills/ With their camels," soon to arrive.

The Little People of "A Rhapsody on Irish Themes" (where Jarrell's Irish great-grandmother holds out to him in dream a dollar bill he is told is "A handkerchief manufactured with their own hands/ By the Little People") enter into the nativity pageant as miniature angels on the crossbeams facing the church-like stable housing the placid ox and ass, "two heads in the manger/ So much greater than the human head, who also adore." The choice of the pronoun *who* personifies these brothers of men to fit in with their prospect of beatitude when the natural world will be made new—a concept of Saint Paul, for whom Randall Jarrell had a lasting devotion. Five more angels hover "in midair like hummingbirds," and two tiara-bedecked angelic twins with auburn hair in blue garments balance a white-robed pair painted in profile near the symbolic offering of wheat, lilies, iris, and columbine "front stage": a still life in a deeper meaning than the painter's definition of that genre, an outward sign of the "timeless moment" when Christ was born of Mary.

The presence of all nineteen angels in the middle panel is integrative, underlining its message, the primacy of the Incarnation in the linear history of humanity. Slightly varying the de La Tour's "the one thing in the world," Jarrell moves away from the tableau of mourners to the jubilance of "The time of the world concentrates/ On this one instant." Already he has introduced the compelling power of "the naked/ Shining baby, like the needle of the compass," an affirmative variant on the North Pole of "90 North," about which Suzanne Ferguson writes: "the beginning of all lines, the beginning of 'meaning,' since one locates oneself on earth by relation to it" (p. 20). This "still point" has attracted the past, as in the first panel where Joseph assists Mary over harsh-looking rocks under leafless trees while the donkey walks behind; it will attract the future, not only the Wise Men being directed to the stable in the third panel at top, but also those who like Jarrell study the Van der Goes donor kneeling in the changelessness of art.

A walk through any art gallery requires stepping from Christocentric rooms of medieval and Renaissance piety into celebrations of field, ocean, sky over forests, of nudes, of flower-and-fruit arrangements popular in early modern periods, to festivals of color and juxtaposed geometric forms wherein not only "Christ disappears, the dogs disappear," as "The Old and the New Masters" says, but all that is recognizable in the visible universe is replaced by invention. Jarrell speaks of the beginning of this trend in "the masters show the crucifixion/ In one corner of the canvas," though which masters he has in mind among those who flourished as Humanism took over are unknown. At a meeting of the American Federation of Art in Houston in 1957, he offered a spirited rebuttal to Meyer Shapiro's eulogy on nonrepresentation, his opposition based on the ideas in the *Art News* essay, "The Art of the Chimpanzee":

In the symposium that followed, poet Randall Jarrell violently attacked Abstract Expressionism, calling it the "intensive exploitation of one part of the revolutionary tradition of Bonnard, Matisse and Picasso . . ." In essence he called for a return to nature, declaring that "Man and the world are all that they ever were."[19]

The last painting that "The Old and the New Masters" treats explicitly is Paolo Veronese's enormous canvas now known as *Christ in the House of Levi*, housed in the Accademia of Venice, a city where Veronese is ranked second only to Titian. The subject of biblical feasts had always intrigued this artist: a painting in Turin celebrates the banquet that Simon the Pharisee made for Jesus, and *The Marriage at Cana* was done in 1563 for the Benedictine Church San Giorgio Maggiore, a work as devoid of supernatural content as "Dance Figure" on the same wedding, a lovely short poem written by Ezra Pound in his "young years," Pound who, in 1972, had his funeral Mass in this very same Venetian church.

Sixteenth-century art patrons frowned upon subjectivity in the depiction of the life of Jesus. It was not extraordinary, then, that Veronese's 1573 entertainment of Christ by Levi stirred up an ecclesiastical controversy. Jarrell summarizes the dispute in "The new masters paint a subject as they please,/ And Veronese is persecuted by the

Inquisition/ For the dogs playing at the feet of Christ." Originally, the painter had intended a *Last Supper:* at the midpoint, the Lord is engaged in casual conversation with John, who is placed at his left hand in defiance of tradition, while Peter, suspicious of their interchange, cranes his neck from the other side of Jesus in an attempt to overhear. There is no trace of the solemn institution of the Eucharist in this crowded banquet hall, completely divorced through its classical architecture from the New Testament setting of the upper room. Unrepentant before his accusers, Veronese capitulated to the extent of giving his Holy Thursday scene a neutral title, *Christ in the House of Levi,* rather than make the changes ordered by the court to be done within three months, changes incompatible with the artist's professional conscience.

Though a guessing game, "Name the Poet," might be played with unidentified passages from Wordsworth and Wallace Stevens, such as "The light that never was on land and sea" and "The vivid transparence that you bring is peace," no one could ever mistake Randall Jarrell's poetic idiom, particularly in the final, or "Lost World," phase, for that of any previous century. As "The Old and the New Masters" finishes its brief art history, he makes the assertion in plain speech, with a scientific ring, that "The earth is a planet among galaxies." The masters who have succeeded theocentric and then homocentric painters surpass the most outlandish wizards of science fiction, to which Jarrell was addicted, as they turn each canvas into "a horde of destructions." These sorcerers have dehumanized the universe to the extent that it is only a diagram wherein this earth, once "so beautiful, so various, so new," has become a fiery cinder, its death going on "somewhere in a corner," as did the Crucifixion in art after the High Renaissance. Abstract Expressionists embody the view of art entertained by André Malraux, which Jarrell faults in his résumé of *The Voices of Silence:* "one of conquest, of victory, power, domination" (*A Sad Heart at the Supermarket,* p. 176). Their age, his own, was one in which he felt increasingly uncomfortable, even though in a Harvard lecture he blamed public taste for condemning nonrepresentational art (*Poetry and the Age,* p. 10).

VI   *"In Galleries"*

The last major poetic treatment of museum art, "In Galleries," begins with one of the "sparrows" watched over by Providence, a guard in gray uniform—even his hair "uniformly gray"—a drab character somehow endeared to the reader by Jarrell's never-failing ability to feel with others. Using "you" as the focus of narration, the poet enters the semi-consciousness of this guard who is "blind," though not physically as his Italian counterpart, later in the poem, *is* physically dumb. The guardian of treasures has become deadened through the years by the indifference of the visitors to whom he is no more than "a reflection" or thought, to be walked through. Though the laughing stone Infant tickled by Mary moves the spectators, its guard's humanity has disappeared into the background until he is truly as invisible as Ralph Ellison's hero. Mary Jarrell identifies Jarrell's source of imagery here as Agostino di Duccio's fifteenth-century relief *Virgin and Child*, in the same museum in Florence as Donatello's *David*.

The Jarrell family spent the summer of 1960 in Italy with Peter and Eleanor Taylor. Taylor was "the most fiercely devoted friend anyone ever had," Jarrell once told Lane Kerr, assistant editor of the *Greensboro Daily News*, who recalled the praise in that paper on October 16, 1965, two days after the poet's death.

Quite likely the Jarrells with or without the Taylors visited Rome during this vacation, though the second stanza of "In Galleries" may have had another genesis during an earlier or later trip to Italy. The masterpiece to which this section is devoted is the "Ludovisi Throne," located in the Terme Museum. Dated before the Golden Age of Praxiteles, the magnificent piece, in view of the weight of the material, was probably carved by some itinerant Ionian sculptor rather than brought from Greece to the Ludovisi Villa near Rome, where it was discovered. Even though this three-sided relief has been known through the ages as the "Ludovisi Throne," it was very likely designed to be part of an altar.

Randall Jarrell's interest in the Anadyomene motif in art has already been explored in "The Birth of Venus." This Roman sculpture pictures the same scene as Botticelli's Uffizi Venus, the goddess of love "just rising from the sea waves, for her tunic clings wetly to her body, and the pebbly shore is suggested under the feet of the Horae on either side of her."[20] The priestesses, broken off at the shoulderline, wait eternally to shelter their patronal deity, whose raised countenance and extended arms have none of the reluctance to enter Time expressed in Botticelli's *Nascita di Venere*. The other two sides show Earthly Love as a handmaiden offering incense, and Heavenly Love, a naked damsel with crossed legs (the posture of the best Kannons in Buddhist sculpture) who sits on a cushion playing a double flute, like Robert Creeley's Koré. The nudity of the flautist anticipates that joy in the human form char-

acteristic of Periclean Greece, recalling the *David*'s anticipation of late
Renaissance portrayals of Adam's sons and daughters in undraped
freedom.

Near the "Ludovisi Throne" in the Museo delle Terme is a mutilated
Aphrodite. The guard is afraid, in Jarrell's presentation of him, that
the American visitors will miss it:

> And exclaiming hopefully, vivaciously,
> *Bellissima!* he shows you that in the smashed
> Head of the crouching Venus the untouched lips
> Are still parted hopefully, vivaciously,
> In a girl's clear smile.

By the repetition, Venus's hope and vivacity are also attributed to this
shabby guard, so courageous before the disappointments and routine
of life. Praising Jarrell's flatness of language, Donald Stauffer says about
a later passage: "Only a poet with great skill and daring craftsmanship
could arrange these seven nonstop lines [ending in 'are dumbly one']
about a guard in an Italian art museum in a way to make the climax
seem inevitable."[21]

In stanza three of "In Galleries," the poet refers to the *Madonna of
the Pietà*, in the Castelvecchio Museum in Verona, according to Mary
Jarrell in a letter to the author in December 1977. The magnifying
glass held by the kind guard reveals its minute miraculous detail, a
single tear of Mary shining on the arm of her Son after the Crucifixion,
as she holds in her arms "the death of the world," an echo from the
opening of the poem, where she held in her arms the Child who was
its life as well as its death (" . . . God/ Being tickled by the Madonna;
the baby laughs/ And pushes himself away from his mother.").

The introspection wherein Randall Jarrell perceives his own perception of this artifact, the Verona painting, creates a new "composition"
based on a poem he must often have taught, Wallace Stevens's "Thirteen Ways of Looking at a Blackbird."[22] Too close for coincidence, Jarrell's "fourteenth way," springing from his emotion at the magnifying
of "The something on the man's arm" which is "the woman's/ Tear,"
is " . . . you and the man and the woman and the guard / Are dumbly
one," which must be related to the fourth Stevens fragment, "A man
and a woman and a blackbird/ Are one." The dumbness of the guard
is elevated to a kind of aesthetic and religious inarticulateness (de La
Tour's famous stasis) that catches up into its silence Jarrell himself,

uniting guard and tourist with Mary and Christ in so poignant a way
that one feels beneath the configuration a sincere belief in Christianity
on the part of both guard and poet. Reared in Methodism in Nashville,
Jarrell during his final Easter took communion in the Episcopalian
denomination, but it is to his poetry that one needs to look for answers
to that question once posed by the Messiah to his friends: "What think
you of me?"

VII   *The Significance of Jarrell's Interest in Renaissance Art*

Other examples of Renaissance sculpture in Jarrell's poems include
*The Last Judgment* of the tympanum in the Portal of the Princes in
Bamberg's thirteenth-century cathedral: it is the subject of the brief
"Bamberg," which he wrote in the last year of his life. The first six out
of its nine lines read:

> You'd be surprised how much, at
> The Last Judgment,
> The powers of concentration
> Of the blest and damned
> Are improved, so that
> Both smile exactly alike . . .

This observation is as paradoxical as Germaine Bazin's on this tympanum in *The History of World Sculpture:* "The figures representing
the saved display a euphoric joy rather than an angelic and heavenly
smile, and their candid, mischievous laughter suggests a Paradise filled
with earthly pleasures—as the reward for a life based on those pleasures."[23] In *Pictures from an Institution,* Jarrell likens Gertrude's smile
to "the smiles of the damned at Bamberg" (p. 65). One is reminded of
the end of Flannery O'Connor's "Revelation," where the "sinners"
leap joyfully first into heaven, while the righteous soberly bring up the
end of the rainbowed procession.

Even more significant to Jarrell among Germanic stone monuments
is the Nativity in the cathedral at Augsburg. This is another exercise in
adoration, a subject whereon the Old Masters differ as here the anonymous carver differs from Van der Goes in meditating upon the birth
of Jesus. Jarrell strikes the word *stone* over and over in the lyric: "the
child nursing at the stone/ Breast beside a stone ox, stone ass" ("The
Augsburg Adoration"). He continues this musical effect of the sound

*stone* in "The Three Kings/ Bring him stones and stones and stones,"
contrasting with the seeming permanence the not-so-transient sparrow
which, from the building of the cathedral until the day when as trav-
eller the poet seeks out Augsburg "To adore something," has offered
its unfailing gift of straw, new with each repetitive sparrow as the stone
itself, wearing away, is not new.

Set against a sculpted Bethlehem, the little sparrow is as common a
denominator across the globe as Queen Anne's Lace. The nondescript
bird unites not only Ulm to Greensboro but the present moment to the
time of the Caesars ("The green Forum's sparrows are the sparrows of
home"). It draws into this simultaneity Palestine itself, where Jesus
immortalized the sparrow in the sentence rendered by the King James
version, used by Jarrell, as *"One of these* [the poet substitutes *them*]
*shall not fall/ On the ground without your Father."*

While no Miniver Cheevy (his reputation as a nondrinker would
preclude that), Randall Jarrell seems in some respects more suited to
the heroic days of "iron clothing" than to the computerized society he
reacted against in *A Sad Heart at the Supermarket.* His sensibility
leads him to prefer a Renaissance mask just as surely as Pound in "His-
trion." Like his nineteenth-century idol, Goethe, he looked backward
in time, at least in these analogies with art, for his inspiration. He is no
more just a voice of his own age than Goethe's *Faust* is an exponent of
the *Sturm und Dräng* period wherein it was written. Jarrell's fondness
for the Renaissance as incarnated into art caused him to cherish its
works, such as Uccello's *The Battle of San Romano* (cf. *Pictures*, p.
143), brought back to him in a good reproduction by his friend Robert
Lowell after a trip to Italy. As for Brueghel, he kept a copy of *Hunters
in the Snow* in his office, in addition to the one in "the little house in
the woods."

Like Goethe, Randall Jarrell had almost superhuman versatility, a
mark of that intelligence which was the wonder of all his associates,
and a Renaissance curiosity as well as desire for excellence, ranging
from athletics, fashions, and sports cars to classical ballet, music, and
painting. He fits the passage wherein Ophelia recalls the Hamlet she
knew before his mission of revenge disordered his princely qualities.
Harold Jantz in *Goethe's Faust as a Renaissance Man: Parallels and
Prototypes* quotes the German writer as saying in 1826: "As long as
the poet merely expresses his own few objective perceptions, he cannot
be called a poet but as soon as he knows how to make the world his
own and to express it, he is a poet."[24] Jarrell knew how to, and was.[25]

Reviewing for the *Times Literary Supplement*, March 24, 1978, S. S. Prawer expresses Jarrell's passion for Goethe thus:

> One cannot read far into the works of the late Randall Jarrell without becoming aware now fascinated he was, all through his brief career as poet, critic, and novelist, by the writings and the personality of Goethe. His very first volume of literary criticism, *Poetry of [sic] the Age,* is studded with admiring references to, and unhackneyed quotations from, Goethe's poetry and prose. . . . And then, of course, there is *Pictures from an Institution,* that witty and compassionate novel in which the narrator and the sympathetic Dr. Rosenbaum vie with one another in quoting Goethe with approval (p. 338).

Though largely dissatisfied with Jarrell's "translation," Prawer feels that in it he has produced "a new, and often delightful, work of art," as indeed was the poet's intention as he sought to add to the laurels of (and make more accessible) his Renaissance hero. The objectivity accorded personal insight by the choice of great art as the foundation for poetry has given direction to those of his age such as W. D. Snodgrass (who declares Jarrell the leading influence on his own work), author of six poems on paintings about which he spoke in 1977 at the Chrysler Museum, Norfolk, Virginia.

No reason for Jarrell's devotion to *Faust* strikes one as more relevant than this further comment by Harold Jantz: "We should turn to it [*Faust*] not to learn precepts for life but to learn life" (p. 136). Goethe had an uncanny ability to enter into the Renaissance. The heart of the Renaissance is Man; and into the heart of Man, in poem after poem, Randall Jarrell also enters.

# CHAPTER 5

## *The Original Bat-Poet*

THE preceding chapters on Jarrell's poetry intimate rather than exhaust his multifaceted genius. A third could readily follow on those lyrics that involve the Old and the New Testaments, the most interesting being the autobiographical mask entitled "Jonah," as well as others on different themes. Since he himself constructed list after list of preferences in his reviews, there is excuse for singling out some favorites not treated in detail ahead: "Losses," "Hohensalzburg: Fantastic Variations on a Theme of Romantic Character," "The Carnegie Library, Juvenile Division," "The Woman at the Washington Zoo," "The Sleeping Beauty: Variation of the Prince," "The Girl Dreams that She Is Giselle," "A Soul," "A Sick Child," "Cinderella," "Nestus Gurley," "The Black Swan," "Deutsch durch Freud," "The End of the Rainbow." Like his own "top-billings," the catalog is no sooner ended than seen as flawed by omissions. Yet its concreteness highlights the power of this poet to change.

On *The Nashville Tennessean*'s literary page, where fifty years earlier Donald Davidson was acquainting the South with the Fugitives, Thomas Inge has called for a study to reveal Jarrell as the supreme poet he was: "But the time is ripe for someone to come forth and state with the proper justification and support—a careful analysis of his style and technique as an inspired craftsman—that Randall Jarrell was one of the two or three at the very top of his generation as a contemporary American poet."[1]

Meanwhile, a self-portrait of Jarrell the poet emerges from the triad of children's books on which he had the good luck to collaborate with another "poet," Maurice Sendak.

Sendak, in his remarks to a session of the National Council of Teachers of English, meeting in New York in November 1977, made the same suggestion, recognizing how self-revelatory of the writer was this triad for which they had planned the "decorations." He reported that his own original books, especially *Where the Wild Things Are*, were "super-personal"; so he regarded Randall's, unified by the theme of the search for a mother and rising from that "primitive place," the subconscious, locus of a child's paradise which is "truer than time." Despite the war lyrics, Jarrell by temperament was no hawk, but "a small, furred animal," like the little brownish bat he chose as his symbol in the best-known of his children's books.

No partnership could have been more felicitous than that of Jarrell and Sendak. At first, the artist objected to the proposal that he illustrate Randall's *The Bat-Poet*, feeling that the lyrics were illustration enough entirely apart from the exquisitely pictorial effects in the prose. Finally he agreed, but only on the terms that his contributions be announced as "pictures by Sendak," as they are on the dust jacket. In Jarrell he found a keen graphic sense (in his earlier years, the poet had executed representational paintings in warm colors), together with that music which he confesses most stimulates his own work.[2] Their business relationship grew into friendship, shared by Mary Jarrell, with whom they went places in New York when not working: "I loved Randall Jarrell," Sendak told the English teachers at the meeting mentioned above.

After the poet died, Maurice Sendak continued "decorating" (his own word) Jarrell's books. An example is his posthumous designs for *The Golden Bird and Other Tales from Grimm*. Four stories had appeared in 1962 in a volume also containing Lore Segal's renditions of others. Introducing a different version of the Grimm tales, that by Sandro Nardini, Jarrell noted: "I know a poet who has written poems about Hansel and Gretel, Sleeping Beauty, the Frog Prince, and Cinderella."[3] The poet was, of course, himself.

Jarrell used at least thirty-six of the Grimm fairy stories in his lyrics. "Cinderella" casts into symbol an unhappy marriage in the way that moderns tend to use the Medusa myth, as Samuel French Morse did in "Beyond Medusa."[4] Had Sendak decorated Randall's prose translation of "Cinderella," he might have put in an enormous cat with fierce eyes, glowering from the hearth at the maiden and her newly met godmother, a pair who, smiling like two old women, "lapped in each other's looks,/ Mirror for mirror, drank a cup of tea." In the tales he did do, the images seem suggested by Jarrell: the dog with his stern disapproving stare at the witch in "Hansel and Gretel" (more prominent than the children); the owl as ominous center of Snow White's story; the puppy in bed with his fisherman-master as the greedy wife stands over them to pronounce her final wish. In fact, Maurice Sendak affirms he can still hear Randall Jarrell's voice in the room with him whenever he works on one of the stories.

## I   The Bat-Poet

No one knew more intimately than Mary Jarrell the blessedness of the Sendak-Jarrell team. Reviewing *The Animal Family*, she comments thus:

> Mr. Sendak's unique illustrations are a kind of music you hear while you read. It is a strange music made of pines and shells and misshapen cliffs and it comes from moonlight and ocean waves and deserted places. They belong with the book as much as the book belongs with the sentence of Gogol's that my husband quotes for the preface: 'Say what you like, but such things do happen—not often, but they do happen.'[5]

And no one guessed more wrongly about children's reactions to the initial book, *The Bat-Poet*, than Hayden Carruth: "The kids won't like it and I don't blame them."[6] The fact that it is still going strong in paperback as well as hard cover editions is proof enough of his error. While the charm and depths of *The Bat-Poet* dawned gradually on reviewers, some acclaimed it at once, such as Lavinia Ross, who attributes to it the immortality that Ingmar Bergman felt his films to possess: she quotes Bergman as saying, "After seeing my pictures, I hope people will see a little more—the light will change—the landscape will look a little different."[7] It did, after Jarrell.

When *The Bat-Poet* appeared, dust jacket and frontispiece showed a "solitary singer," not the thrush with which Whitman identified himself in "Out of the Cradle Endlessly Rocking," but a small creature "like a furry mouse with wings." The simple adventures of this "little light brown bat" are those of Jarrell himself, in their essence. No sensitive child or adult would mistake the Bat-poet for just a bat, any more than the Mole as only mole in *The Wind in the Willows*. Shortly after Jarrell's death, this identity was acknowledged by a North Carolina journalist: "But 'The Bat-Poet,' like 'Alice in Wonderland,' is more than a children's story. It is the story of the Bat-Poet who for a long time to come, will remain one of America's greatest living poets,"[8] the second adjective ironical but accurate.

Beginning the bat-parable "Once upon a time" lifts it out of the ordinary. As Thomas Noesen says in "Fairy Tales and the Gospels," this standard opening causes time to disappear in favor of an eternal dimension: "Whether we say 'once upon a time' as in the fairy tale or 'in the beginning' as in John's gospel, we have expressed the same point in history: no point."[9] The story goes beneath sequential "facts" into something more important: a totality of message. The use of "you" introduces an auditor, perhaps Mary, to whom the book is dedicated. Like a *doppelgänger*, Jarrell goes in and out of the little house, studying the bats over his head and occasionally turning a flashlight on them to watch them screw up their faces in the painful glare. His presence as character and audience in the drama achieves aesthetic distance.

When the fable begins, the coffee-colored bat is as wingless in daylight as the others in the bunch hanging upside-down from the porch rafters, but gradually, unlike the rest, he experiments with the sun. With summer's end, the other bats having retreated to the barn, he finds himself alienated; pleading with them to return but meeting refusal, he no more succumbs to following them than did his creator to following the popular tastes he deprecated in *A Sad Heart at the Supermarket*. Like Jonathan Seagull, he decides to "go it alone."[10] Loneliness often afflicted Randall Jarrell. Autumn having arrived, the bat-poet is seized with this emotion: "So he had to sleep all alone. He missed the others." But he bravely accepts his fate of nonconformist.

In the hitherto unknown daytime world, he makes friends with other animals and birds, the most satisfactory being the chipmunk, a parallel to Mary Jarrell in its appreciation of his poetry. Jarrell's interest in Marianne Moore, translator of La Fontaine and deviser of many original fabulae, shines forth in the types of persons represented by the bat's new acquaintances.[11] In *Poetry and the Age*, he compares her lyrics to animals that rescue "the foolish heroes of fairy tales—which can save only the heroes, because they are too small not to have been disregarded by everyone else" (p. 166).

As the bat-poet admits into his ken the squirrels, chipmunks, possums, and owls whose lives he has previously slept through, his vision is extended, as poets' must be before their readers' vision can be. He comes to "see" in the sense of "understand" how shadows can be "bright as moonlight" and how the "black-and-gray turns to green-and-gold-and-blue," knowledge locked away from his somnolent bat-relatives. In the "blurred and golden" light he perceives how the chipmunk's tail is rosy and in his poem likens the color to maple leaves and fox fur. In short, as he comes to live a multicolored existence, his poetic ability strengthens ("the sunlight and the shadows and the red and yel-

low and orange branches made a kind of blurred pattern . . ."). Arrived
at the gift of thinking in landscapes ("In the west, over the gray hills
the sun was red"), he discovers the sunset forever hidden from the
other bats.

In "The Obscurity of the Poet" Jarrell laments over how most persons of his age, having read neither the poetry of yesterday nor of
today, cannot understand "the mockingbird's song," nor have they any
wish to try (*Poetry and the Age*, p. 3). The bat-poet's plea to the polite
but uninterested other bats that they listen to the mockingbird (a good
poet, despite a difficult personality) reminds one of Jarrell's desire that
everyone enjoy the poetry *he* enjoyed: "Once you get used to [the
mockingbird's song] it sounds wonderful." In real life, whether in a
conference with a student or in letters to friends like Taylor and Lowell, he would say about their original verse "It's wonderful . . .
Wonderful!" just as the little bat does, listening to the virtuosity of the
mockingbird. In the fable, the mockingbird, possibly representing the
New Critics, offers only dry comments on line-lengths and metrical
dexterity as response to the timid bat's first song.

The bat's imitative period, patterned on a number of poets as recap-
itulated in the mockingbird's music (Auden, Yeats, Tate, Warren),
coincides with *Blood for a Stranger*, its words often too derivative to
be united in an original "tune." As his apprenticeship continues, he
sees in a flash of insight that "If you get the words right you don't need
a tune." The poetic career of the bat-poet is not all advances, any more
than was Jarrell's: there were times when only translations were possible and when the dread of never recovering poetic powers was heavy
upon him. His own misgivings appear in *The Bat-Poet:* "But sometimes the poem would seem so bad to him that he'd get discouraged
and stop in the middle, and by the next day he'd have forgotten it."
Sometimes too he began a prose work he found impossible to complete:
the way the cardinal resisted the bat-poet's Muse as a subject has its
parallel in Hart Crane, on whom Jarrell once undertook to do a small
book, financed by a Guggenheim grant. Though he greatly admired
Crane, difficulty after difficulty intervened, until finally he had to give
up the project and return the money. In *The Bat-Poet* his friend the
chipmunk encourages him about the verse-portrait he is struggling to
do on the cardinal: "Why, just say what he's like, the way you did
about the owl and me," yet try as best he can the bat-poet cannot put
into words the beauty of the cardinal.

The villain of this Jarrellian fable enters the action early, in an episode which almost resulted in the demise of the "hero": one night an owl swoops toward him, coming so close that the little bat would have been caught had not a refuge offered itself in the hole in the old oak growing beside the little house in the wood, a symbolic salvation by the Sacred Wood of Sir James Frazer and Robert Graves. This owl provides the subject for "The Bird of Night," possibly the most suitable lyric in *The Complete Poems* for introducing Randall Jarrell to high school or college students. Its context, *The Bat-Poet*, while helping as motivation, is not indispensable: the lyric floats free from the fable, as free as its owl-hunter floats over and through the woods. Robert Penn Warren's "The Owl," one of his lesser-known pieces, and his "Time as Hypnosis" make excellent comparative studies, since all three are initiations into the problem of evil, along with Warren's "Blackberry Winter." "Thinking of the Lost World" is another such initiation, the grandmother attacking the chicken taking the place of the owl.

Jarrell's traumatic exposure to the "murder" of that chicken haunted him throughout life, nor is it absent from the owl-poem (p. 12) that the bat-poet, inspired by the mockingbird, composes:

> A shadow is floating through the moonlight.
> Its wings don't make a sound.
> Its claws are long, its beak is bright.
> Its eyes try all the corners of the night.
>
> It calls and calls: all the air swells and heaves
> And washes up and down like water.

As in Warren's "Bearded Oaks," an Atlantis metaphor prevails: *floating, swells, heaves, washes, water*. The liquidity of the consonants heightens the effect, as does the undulating imitative not only of the ocean but also of easy flight. The moonlight itself is the "water."

Moonlight is used so often in Jarrell that it might be thought of as a character binding the lyrics together in a narrative way, just as the same person appears throughout thirty feet of a Chinese scroll on life along a river. In "Hohensalzburg: Fantastic Variations on a Theme of Romantic Character," the invisible vampire, who says *"I am here behind the moonlight,"* may be nothing but the moonlight. Other examples that significantly employ moonlight are "A Girl in a Library," "The Märchen," "The Rising Sun," "Windows," "A Ward in the States," "Mother, Said the Child," "Hope," "Dreams," "A Ghost

Story." Sendak's double-page picture (pp. 6–7) closest to "The Bird of Night" shows owl and moon prominently in conjunction.

To imagine the bird as a floating shadow with wings is original and beautiful. In the line drawing opposite the poem, Maurice Sendak suggests in the wings the headdress of an Indian chief, silhouetted against the disc of moon and centered in the only clear area in the wilderness, with its ivy, gnarled trees, leafy branches, ferns, grasses. The polysyllabic meter of "A shadow is floating in the moonlight" gives way in the second line to the retardation of the three strong stresses "wings don't make." In the third, the shadow has not only wings but claws and beak; the doom of small furry creatures hiding below is not ameliorated by the adjective *bright*, alliterating with *beak*, since the brightness may be blood. The caesura, part of the leisurely flight, helps the hunter to scrutinize his terrain.

Besides claws and beak, this shadow is equipped with eyes that "try" all the corners of the night, turning the forest from huge seaweed clusters and coral to a new metaphor, a prison from which there is no escape, the "corners" implying its rectangular shape. The onomatopoeic identical rhyme—"It calls and calls: all the air swells and heaves"—is common in Jarrell. When the mockingbird evaluates the bat's poem he does not mention the repetition of the letter *l* here, leading up to and away from *all*, that word so common in Jarrell lyrics, though it is the sort of thing he does notice, to the author's dismay, instead of the fright at the heart of the composition.

No ear, of itself, believes in death; to say so is metonymy. But poets do and none more so than Randall Jarrell, from *Blood for a Stranger* through *The Lost World*. Although not specifically occurring in this stanza, as in "Lady Bates," the hooting of the owl vibrates so threateningly through the air that it seems to own it: the night becomes "the owl's air," meant on a secondary level as mournful melody ("If you get the words right you don't need a tune"). "Still as death" could be trite, but next to "stone" and when attributed to the scared little mouse and the even more scared (because more aware) bat, it is no cliché. The quiet ocean of moonlight become a prison, now as if in a Charles Burchfield painting, turns into a living creature that can hold its breath in terror, the cutting off of the final line dramatizing this fear, as the mockingbird notes: "And it was clever of you to have that last line two feet short" (p. 14). The mood is unlike the calm acceptance of the companion-piece ("The Breath of Night") from a 1947 *Kenyon Review*, though even this poem detects beneath the joy of the forest's beauty at night "the Strife that moves the stars." The universe itself in "The Bird of Night" trembles before the owl.

Maurice Sendak's theory, alluded to above, is that the "search for a mother" ties together *The Bat-Poet, The Animal Family,* and *Fly by Night.* This motif was already present in *The Gingerbread Rabbit,*[12] illustrated by Garth Williams. Its most direct elucidation in the first Sendak volume is the fourth poem: "Sleepily, almost dreaming, the bat began to make up a poem about a mother and her baby." Like W. C. Williams, Jarrell believed the unconscious to be the place where poems are born: in "Dreams" "The darkness puts to its lips its finger./ The children spell in their sleep." In the magical state of dream the bat recalls the story of his own infancy: "It was easier than the other poems somehow: all he had to do was remember what it had been like and every once in a while put in a rhyme," like Wallace Stevens striking the silver chime of a rhyme at will.

Jarrell's mother died shortly after he did, early in 1966, the following year. Although very close when he was a child, they grew apart. Yet there was a time when as a young boy in California he wrote affectionate, funny, "sharing" letters to her in Tennessee, enjoying a relationship he idealizes in that of the little bat and his mother, one quite different from the estrangement described as early as "The Bad Music," which must have been written in the 1930s. Here, he remembers his mother as crying; the son asks, " . . . how many know or love at all/ You, Anna?" about her present status and answers himself, "Enough." *The Animal Family* underscores that happy memories of Anna were not dead; in fact, one is recalled in "The Player Piano," where Jarrell, disguised as a feminine speaker, writes, "I remember how I'd brush my mother's hair/ Before she bobbed it."

The bat's birth is in human terms, "Naked and blind and pale." The poem he makes up about himself, like "The Bird of Night," simulates flight: "Doubling and leaping, soaring, somersaulting. . . ." The baby bat hangs on underneath the mother's body. About a third of the thirty-four lines rhyme, and about a third are in pentameter, but shorter line-lengths dominate to give the illusion of flying. The figures of speech—for example, "Like shining needlepoints of sound"—make up in quality for quantity. In the embroidery image (the synesthetic needle of the "high sharp cries" of the mother bat weaving in and out of the moonlight-and-shadow fabric) the poet "complicates" in the way that the original bat-poet loved to: it is a compass reference, a variant of the Christ Child toward which everything is pointed in "The

Old and the New Masters" ("The naked,/ Shining baby, like the needle of a compass"). The seventeenth line is followed by a pivot, the "echo" trick Jarrell had praised in *Paterson*, here "In full flight; in full flight." In Sendak's picture for the poem, love stands in antithesis to death: "Their single shadow, printed on the moon/ Or fluttering across the stars,/ Whirls on all night." Home again, the mother like a guardian angel "folds her wings about her sleeping child."

In H. W. Suber one sees a reviewer who early detected the personal revelation that Sendak was to note: "Randall Jarrell, in his book 'The Bat-Poet, left an autobiography of sorts."[13] But this children's tale also serves as a literary memoir, Suber believes, a critique of the age itself, alluding obliquely to Robert Frost ("After Apple Picking"), to Dylan Thomas ("Fern Hill"); besides being "an annotated anthology of the Bat-Poet's [Jarrell's] own poems" and "a textbook on contempoetics," it can also be taken as "an introduction to Ezra Pound." The author of *Personae* may well be the mockingbird, assuming one voice after another (Daniel, Browning, Villon). In the lyric on the mockingbird which the bat sings to the chipmunk, he may be satirizing Pound's youthful role among fellow-writers from his posts as foreign editor in Europe: "On the willow's highest branch, monopolizing/ Day and night, cheeping, squeaking, soaring," and again, "All day the mockingbird has owned the yard" and "fighting hard/ To make the world his own" (p. 28). If this be true, the genuine admiration with which Jarrell regarded *The Cantos* nevertheless comes through at the end:

> A mockingbird can sound like anything.
> He imitates the world he drove away
> So well that for a minute, in the moonlight,
> Which one's the mockingbird? which one's the world?

If Randall Jarrell wrote little about *il miglior fabbro* ("the better maker"), he did consciously benefit from Poundian technique in such dramatic monologues as "Jonah." As a teacher Jarrell thought each of his Greensboro students better than they were. Similarly he may have been presenting in his generous and persistent eulogies of the mockingbird (Pound?) to the other bats, as well as in his bat-poet discipleship, a much more positive than negative estimate of the poet whom some critics were accusing of vanity, arrogance, over-concern with technique.

## II   The Animal Family

Despite its title, the protagonist of *The Animal Family* is a human being, a hunter who finds a mermaid by following a mysterious song to the ocean near a cabin made of logs which he, like Robinson Crusoe, has chopped down himself. Yet even before he begins to collect his "family" about him, this hunter's garments identify him with animals: deerskin trousers, shirt, and shoes; cloak of a mountain lion's hide; cap of a sea-otter's skin. Moreover, he has ornamented the walls and chairs of his house with foxes, seals, a lynx, a mountain lion, as if to prepare the right kind of home for those who will occupy it. This classic has often been likened to *The Little Prince*, its central character at home amidst the nonhuman. Margaret Sherwood Libby wrote "Not since St.-Exupèry's *Little Prince* have I found a book of this kind that I wanted to share with everyone."[14]

Mary Jarrell relates the setting to their residence on South Lake Drive in Greensboro, though at the same time picturing it as a collage of Randall's memories of drives along the Pacific, scenes from Coos Bay to Big Sur.[15] Mixed in with these recollections are visits to Rock Creek Park in Washington, D.C. But more important than these is the ivied Greensboro house, present also as setting in the other two Sendak books, with its seat under the large eastern window made of stained and clear glass combined. The hunter's possessions in *The Animal Family* were actually Randall's: the brass horn, ship's figurehead, animal pelts, wooden table utensils. The fireplace is the fireplace of the home where this prose-poem dream was dreamed, in the tranquillity of the North Carolina evenings.[16]

The projected essay mentioned above on Randall Jarrell and music could deal not just with the operatic and orchestral, but also with nameless melodies like the one that brings out the mother-motif as the hunter, warm under his bearskin, hears it in the song of the waves: "the great soft sound the waves made over and over. It seemed to him that it was like his mother singing." When he falls off to sleep, it really *is* the mother, sitting by his bed singing. In *The Animal Family*, which opens with the same four words that *The Bat-Poet* does, one is conscious that this lullaby is "once upon a time, long, long ago," partly through the reference to his dead father, who sits repairing bow and arrow at the fireplace. The same dream returns in the summer: when sleep comes, "his thoughts changed to dreams, and his mother was singing to him." When he awakens in the moonlight the mother-figure singing changes to the seal-like creature in the waters, not yet classified as a mermaid. It might be the moonlight itself: in that strange little design by Sendak on the title page the moon is wreathed in leaves, the symbol of the mermaid whose hair and skin Jarrell describes as "the same silvery blue-green, the color of the moonlight on the water." As if she were truly only the moonlight, the mermaid, unlike the person- alities in *The Bat-Poet*, never appears in the decorations.

The bat, once he has discovered the joy of poetry through the mock- ingbird, goes on to original composition; the hunter remains a "mock- ingbird." He courts the mermaid by memorizing a tag of the song from the sea and interspersing it among all the other tunes he can recollect. The speech of human and ondine are mutually unintelligible, but not hopelessly so, any more than the children's after a taste of dragon's blood in "Children Selecting Books in a Library":

> . . . The children's cries
> Are to men the cries of crickets, dense with warmth
> —But dip a finger into Fafnir, taste it,
> And all their words are plain as chance and pain.
> (*C. P.*, p.106)

Gleefully they begin to teach each other, she making many an amusing mistake in language though a quicker learner than he. When she asks what "mistakes" are, Jarrell the hunter replies in a manner applicable to his own poetic practice: "The wrong word—the wrong sound, one you don't mean to make." She puzzles over the ambiguities in human speech, such as "legs" in reference to the hunter and to his table, but readily adds the word *leg* to her vocabulary, like the mermaid in "A Soul," who touches the man's legs as she and her lover sit near the shore: "Yes, here is one,// "Here is the other . . . *Legs* . . . / And they move so?"

"A Soul" features in its initial line a bat as nonconformist as the furry winged protagonist of the child's tale: "It is evening. One bat dances/ Alone, where there were swallows." These sentences could serve as epigram for the entire Sendak "trilogy." Written ten years earlier than the fable about the mermaid, it is a tender little dialogue in six stanzas, in which the mermaid's *thou* approximates the German *du*. That happy "dailiness of life" with which "Well Water" ends characterizes this couple, the "once more" disclosing their habit of meeting at night even though the "thin air" is dangerous to her. Exceptional among mermaids as the bat-poet among bats, she has scales on her breast as well as tail, unlike the ondines of art, but she is even more exceptional in that she has gained a soul by winning the love of a human. The same legend, out of Hans Christian Andersen, forms the groundwork of *The Animal Family*, and as implied in her domestication, the same blessing comes to its mermaid, as their love (the love of friendship) matures.

From time to time the sea-creature of *The Animal Family* returns to her former home under the waves, where she finds it as difficult to tell the other mermen and mermaids about a fire as the bat-poet did to communicate to the other bats what bright shadows were. Their problem can be related to "The Obscurity of the Poet." Like the chipmunk, she has a natural understanding of poetic images, shown by her reaction to the branch of red maple leaves the hunter gives her: "The mermaid looked at it as if she couldn't believe it; she carried it, and stroked it, and said to him lovingly, 'It's the best thing I've ever had in all my life.'" Reading *The Animal Family*, Jarrell's former student Sylvia Wilkinson recalled the day she and others brought him a gift: "I remember how excited he was when we carried him a bunch of red berries we had stolen off a campus branch."[17] If he is the Hunter in the fable, he is also the Mermaid.

The fire, after it burns her, becomes an object of fear like the owl to the chipmunk, bewildering but beautiful. She compares it to a red shell just as she has the meadow flowers to white shells. Sendak has chosen for his cover a shell ringed with leaf-tendrils, as the moon is inside the book. The necklace of gold and green and blue stones from the bottom of the sea that the mermaid presents to the hunter is a "poem," received as such when he repeats to her what she has said to him about the red maple branch.

The theme of the lost mother never vanishes: "The hunter would tell her about his father and mother and the years the three of them had lived there, showing her a little square of lace, his mother's handkerchief; to the hunter and the mermaid it was a great treasure" (p. 49). Since the mermaid is not able to imagine a woman, he carves a statue of his mother for her, and she exclaims at once: "'Why, she's like me!'" (p. 50). Thus through fantasy the hunter recovers the mother for whom has he never ceased to shed invisible tears.

The wealth of fairy tales that the hunter shares with his mate (if one can call her that) comes from his dead mother. It is the mother remembered so fondly from boyhood that Jarrell intends in the wish: "Whenever anything reminded him of his father and mother, you could see that he missed them and longed to have them alive again." (In the last of the series, *Fly by Night*, he does resurrect them.)

Since they cannot be parents without a child, the man and mermaid add to their household a bear cub. Sendak's leafless branches reach out as if in love, under the title of Chapter Three, "The Hunter Brings Home a Baby." As always in his decorations for this book, the members of the animal family do not appear. Nothing seems unusual about the bear's entrance into their household circle, though his coming occasions some funny incidents, such as the mermaid's consternation at his hibernation, which recalls to her the mother's Sleeping Beauty story as told her by the hunter. In Chapter Five the man steals a lynx as brother for their son, no doubt a compliment to Elfie, Jarrell's tortoise-shell cat, to whom this volume is dedicated. The newcomer destroys with his sharp claws the mother's lace handkerchief, but it is marvelously repaired, as if in a Hawthorne myth. At the end of this chapter comes a deft foreshadowing of the next when the hunter tells the mermaid how his mother used to admonish their cat "Velvet" to get him to tuck in his claws: "That's what my mother used to say on the boat.'"

The child Jarrell is externalized in the shipwrecked boy found one day by the lynx: "A woman was lying at the other end [of the unlucky vessel], half in and half out of the water that filled the bottom of the boat": huddled against her was a little boy who was crying. Between lynx and bear the boy is installed in the seaside Eden which the cabin has become. When the mermaid and hunter return, they seem scarcely even surprised at finding the sleeping child snuggled up to the bear beside the fireplace. The child's first word to the mermaid when he awakens is "Mama." The burial of the mother that same day by the hunter reawakens in him his own desolation at being parentless. Suspense continues to build as to whether the mermaid will go back to the ocean, as Matthew Arnold's does in "The Forsaken Merman," a poem referred to in "The End of the Rainbow," where a cynic calls mermen only seals and mermaids manatees (aquatic animals with rounded tails). When the mermaid chooses the land as her home, Jarrell uses the decision to say something important about Life, that it is struggle as indeed it is for her—just the opposite of the convent in Hopkins's "Heaven Haven," which is "out of the swing of the sea," where "storms not come."

*The Animal Family* ends in a lie, told to the child by his parents, who have so confused dream and reality in their own minds that they believe their insistence he has always been their child; it is a lie in the sense that art itself is a lie. "We've had you always," are the last words of the book, said by the mermaid to the boy. The symbolic source of this "lie," standing in Jarrell as in Yeats for the creative process, is the seashell and the strange music dwelling within its ivory spiral.

This story offers details from Jarrell's life in the manner that *trobar clus* poetry did in regard to the troubadours. Its most profound autobiographical sense is the whole enchanted world that the family inhabits, the straw of reality spun into gold: "It is not a sentimental happiness. The lynx is stolen from his mother, the boy is cast up by a storm in which *his* mother has died; each of the characters in the fable knows the meaning of pain, and sadness, and fear. But the happiness is there, all the same, though it has to be won."[18] The mermaid must exert effort beyond the usual as she travels without legs to and from the ocean and so does the husband as he tries to decipher her tongue or puts up with her ineptitude in cooking, but somehow they manage, like the young couple in Steinbeck's *The Pearl* who have been driven out of their first paradise only to enter into a more realistic one.[19]

In *The Complete Poems*, the nearest analogue to their marriage is "A Man Meets a Woman in the Street." Sunlight, gingko trees, the wife's hair of coarse gold above her champagne-colored dress all conspire to make the husband happy, though he recognizes mutability. ("if only . . . If only . . ."), especially toward the end:

> After so many changes made and joys repeated,
> Our first bewildered, transcending recognition
> Is pure acceptance. We can't tell our life
> From our wish. Really I began the day
> Not with a man's wish: "May this day be different,"
> But with the birds' wish: "May this day
> Be the same day, the day of my life."
>
> (*C.P.*, p. 353)

If Jarrell's tales begin "Once upon a time," they do not finish "And they lived happily ever after." Yet, as in this poem celebrating conjugal love, they are illuminated with what Robert Penn Warren calls delight.

### III   Fly by Night

*Fly by Night,* concluding the "spiritual autobiography" decorated by Maurice Sendak, did not appear until 1976. The dust jacket shows a mother-figure holding a huge placard on a pole which announces title, author, artist; later in the volume the same woman cradles against herself a child, in the forest "where the wild things are." Never having met Anna Campbell Jarrell Regan, Sendak constructed her out of recollections of his own mother as he drew the dreams of this third "chapter." Also on the jacket, high over the mother's head, the floating David, whose story it is, is pictured face down resting against the air, as if it were the water implied in "The Bird of Night."

The locale is Greensboro, as in the other two books: "If you turn right at the last stoplight on New Garden Road," *Fly by Night* begins. The Jarrells had lived on Spring Lake Drive, which does turn off the New Garden Road cutting through Greensboro. The hero's chow dog is Reddy, the name of the pet rabbit Jarrell had in California as a child (the poet in Part III of "The Lost World" begs his grandmother, "'Mama, you won't kill Reddy ever,/ You won't ever, will you?'" but cannot believe her when she says she would never even think of such a thing). Reddy's worried expression in his prominent righthand corner of the Sendak frontispiece is a transference of the owner's anxiety. David also has a cat named Flour; cats were always indispensable to Jarrell, even in his Nashville days, as remembered by the Breyers.

Nocturnal flying is just the opposite of the accomplishment of the bat-poet, who learns to fly by day, but of course that a boy should fly at all is amazing, like a tree walking. The fact that David is naked, Sendak told the NCTE audience, is to emphasize that there is nothing between him and the experience. After Randall's death, Sendak used the same symbolism in his book *In the Night Kitchen* (New York, 1970) where on the third page Mickey falls through the dark, "out of his clothes," jumping back into them at the end. Randall's devotion to Wordsworth's "Intimations" Ode accords with David's conviction when beginning to float that could he only remember he would have the power always, by day as well as night. The visualization as in comic strip balloons of the dreams of father, mother, dog, sheep is a touch any child-reader would adore. "The End of the Rainbow," possibly Jarrell's own favorite among his lyrics,[20] closes with a similar effect in Su-Su's dream, where like one sheep in *Fly by Night* the animal dreams that he is dreaming:

> The little black dog sleeping in the doorway
> Of the little turquoise store, can dream
> His own old dream: that he is sleeping
> In the doorway of the little turquoise store.
>
> (*C. P.*, p. 229)

The father's dream, wherein he is "running back and forth with David on his back, only David is big as ever, "hints that the son during waking hours may have felt a burden to his father. But it also symbolizes how the child within Jarrell never died. The mother dreams of making pancakes, in a snow of pillow feathers.

As in a Grimm story, or the Acts of the Apostles, the door opens of itself for the hero, who does not seem in the least surprised to have the cat address him in poetry: "Wake by night and fly by night,/ The wood is black,/ the wood is white." Circling within view but out of reach of the cat, three mice also talk in rhyme: "What's that great big black thing in the sky? . . . / It's little David—he can fly." Menaced by the cat, they scamper away into a hole, calling back in an echo of Tatyana's farewell to the girl in the library: "It's time to go—goodbye, goodbye!"

The hypnotic trance of "Lady Bates" returns in the boy's inability to say a word or move, even to yawn or close his eyes. Both trance and dream also recall "Hohensalzburg." Floating over the sheep, he is mingled in image with the girl and her brother of "The Night before the Night before Christmas" ("She and her brother float up from the snow"), though here the only "snow" is fleece in the moonlight.

The main character, outside of David, in the fable is the owl: "It glides towards him silently—then it gives two big slow strokes of its wings, but not a single feather makes a sound." Though the description tallies with the *Bat-Poet's* ("Its wings don't make a sound"), the bird's symbolism is no longer sinister, as if death were taking on a less terrible significance for Jarrell. A silvery fish writhes in its beak, no longer bright with blood but "yellow," the hunter's booty here nothing but a good mother's provision for her nestlings. (The fish as sketched by Sendak for the back cover of the jacket does not look too resigned; rather, it does for the tri-part tale what the skull does for a medieval painting.)

The "search for a mother" motif receives further evidence in the first of the owl's songs, an invitation to David to become for the night one of her offspring. When they arrive at the tree home where the two owlets are waiting and the big silvery fish has been disposed of, the mother owl tells them and David an irregularly rhymed story which takes up five pages of the slender book. This is a fantasy-autobiography of the author, based on the need for a mother: "He'd stand on tiptoe/ Staring across the forest for his mother/ And hear her far away"; the desire for a brother or sister must also have existed in the poet (though Randall did have a brother, Charles, the relationship was severed, except for rare occasions, once their Tennessee boyhood passed, and he had no sister). "The Owl's Bedtime Story" crystallizes remembered loneliness—"Sometimes it seemed to him his heart would break." The cycle comes around to the beginning, the poet as night-creature, bat or owl, in the dreamed white owl's promise of a sister-friend (the mermaid?) if he will fly from the nest "into the harsh unknown/ World the sun lights."

After a series of severe trials, as in the fairy tales, his perseverance in daylight-flying is rewarded by a real owl-sister, not a blood-sister but a beloved substitute (" . . . her face looked dear/ As his own sister's, it was the happiest/ hour of his life." Now he must teach her too to fly in the bright sun. Relevantly, Mary Jarrell is rather clearly meant by "The Meteorite": "Breathe on me still, star, sister";[21] according to her own account she read poems avidly under his tutelage. Imperilled by crows, they wait in a tall tree for rescue by the mother owl: "How strong, how good, how dear/ She did look! 'Mother!' they called in their delight."

The poem about bats in *The Bat-Poet* (p. 37) ends with a mother as guardian angel: "She folds her wings about her sleeping child"; and so does "The Owl's Bedtime Story": "She opened her wings, they nestled to her breast." The next morning David realizes that the shining eyes of the dreamed-owl, as he had suspected the night before, are those of his human mother. The eyes fade into the daylight world, a world in which "his mother looks at him like his mother," the end of *Fly by Night*. It is an echo of "They look back at the leopard like the leopard" in "The Woman at the Washington Zoo."

Sendak's autobiography through his work for children also has its "David" in Max of *Where the Wild Things Are*, who after a night of wild dreams, begun in a bedroom transformed into a forest, sails "back over a year and in and out of weeks and through a day and into the night of his very own room." In Sendak the longing to be the object of a unique affection is phrased thus in the last line of his fantasy: "And Max the king of all wild things was lonely and wanted to be where someone loved him best of all." Being loved "best of all" was more important to Jarrell than it is to most of us. In the "Jerome" worksheets at UNCG,[22] the doctor reaches out for one patient, just one, who will love him for himself and not as surrogate. One likes to think that the poet's loneliness is over now, like the dog Jennie's in a Sendak story "Higgelty Piggelty Pop," published in 1967 two years after Randall's death. Arrived in the Castle Yonder, Jennie sends back a letter to her former master: "As you probably noticed, I went away forever. But if you ever come this way, look for me" (p. 69). The subtitle for this book is "There Must Be More to Life." That "more" was what Randall Jarrell always wanted.

CHAPTER 6

# Critic, Novelist, Translator

JARRELL'S children's books, then, not only mirror the work directed
to adults in so delightful a manner that they can be considered foot-
notes but also form in their longing for absolutes an autobiography second only to this work itself. When he met the Angel of Death that dark
October night near Chapel Hill, he had earned the reputation of first-
rate poet and creator of classics for young readers but he had also
affected the taste of his contemporaries as perhaps no other American
critic has done. His only rivals, Eliot and Pound, had become British
citizen and expatriate, respectively. Among those who remained
behind to practice criticism on their native ground, none surpassed him
in deepening or changing attitudes toward other writers.

His method was to call attention to his enthusiasms in the Augusti-
nian spirit, "Love, so that you may understand." Walt Whitman took
on different significance for a Jarrell-instructed readership, as did sup-
posedly-familiar lyrics by Robert Frost; items of formerly minor poetic
excellence emerged in a hitherto unnoticed poem by Thomas Hardy,
"During Wind and Rain," a choice never again to elude syllabi; William Carlos Williams and other moderns felt with joy the pure appreciation of a disinterested talent. Not all estimates were affirmative:
though chiefly bent on sharing his pleasures, this critic knew how to
use wit to expose what he believed to be mediocre. But above all, he
entertained: no one had realized what fun criticism could be.

Being part of Vanderbilt University so shortly after the heyday of
the Southern Agrarian Fugitives, Randall Jarrell could scarcely escape
having his value judgments affected by their leaders. Allen Tate, the
most prominent of the New Critics in his ambience, affirms this tie in
his Jarrell references throughout the correspondence with Brooks and
Warren as *The Southern Review* editors. Randall was the advisee of
Davidson, the friend and student of Robert Penn Warren. Through the
pages of the Nashville newspaper referred to above, Davidson had
"boomed about" the work of the Agrarians as Pound earlier had that

of Frost and Eliot. He was one of the beginners of *The Fugitive* in the 1920s and a decade later a contributor to their social manifesto, *I'll Take My Stand*. From the tenets this volume builds on, Warren later had to dissociate himself because of its segregationalist outlook; Jarrell, however, decided from the outset that the position was based on too narrow an idea of the art of poetry. Yet *Blood for a Stranger*, if compared with any one of his director Davidson's own books of verse, contains evidence of the older man's impact on metrics and subject, one no more discernible in the mature Jarrell than are the verbal subtleties of his Housman criticism on the later books of essays in criticism.

## I   Poetry and the Age

To go back in time to how Jarrell's first collection of critical essays was received by competent readers, one needs only to refer to F. W. Flint's comments in the November-December, 1953, *Partisan Review*, on "Jarrell as Critic":

Mr. Jarrell is a provoking critic in all senses of the word, one who can be counted on to scatter the unctuous fog which usually surrounds the middle-academic study of letters. He is, or has been, our nearly perfect Jacobin, our Tom Paine of the highbrow quarterlies, keeping alive the great style of the *feuilleton*. (p. 702)

Flint's reservations as he comments on chapter after chapter of *Poetry and the Age* are almost as hard to distinguish from praise as are Jarrell's own in his function as critic, but there is no doubt that he is excited over "the new look" given to the genre by the subject of the book he is reviewing.

Nothing could be further from the worrying of tone, diction, and syntax in the William Empson-dominated "Texts from Housman" than this conversational, startling, often hilarious collection of critical articles published by Jarrell in his fortieth year. By freely sharing both his excitement over certain poems and his disapprobation of others, he "made over" the taste of poetry readers in his own age, winning them to the "old masters" they thought they knew but were used to seeing only through a scrim of standard critical responses, and leading them to look harder at authors "canonized" by Palgrave and other anthologists. His method was that of Matthew Arnold's "touchstones" but used far more exuberantly than by the formal Victorian who introduced this term into the critic's art. Transforming the adage of Alexander Pope, one might say that Randall Jarrell's critical prose exhibited the brilliance of what had ne'er been thought before and therefore ne'er so well expressed.

The book begins with a Harvard lecture, given during a symposium called "The Defense of Poetry." With tongue in cheek, Jarrell named his contribution "The Obscurity of the Poet," whom he does not regard as obscure at all, the "darkness" coming rather from the hostile and handicapped understanding of audiences who refuse to read poetry of any kind; to such, the poet is invisible, "for that corner into which no one looks is always dark" (p. 9). One of his most entertaining and illuminating essays, "The Obscurity of the Poet" wears well through the years, possibly because in its pages wit almost never bends truth to serve cleverness. Unquestionably it shaped preferences after its appearance in 1953: how many, for example, went out to buy or borrow from libraries the one-volume *Remembrance of Things Past* or its multi-volumed French original, after discovering that Randall Jarrell thought Proust the finest writer of the century? Though some of the comments have dated, like that on ventriloquist Edgar Bergen's dummy Mortimer Snerd, on the whole the essay has been as central to modern literary criticism as Eliot's "Tradition and the Individual Talent."

"The Age of Criticism" is its companion-piece in this volume, written in a flowing, informal style, itself the most telling weapon against the pedantry and pomposity of the solemn prose Jarrell is attacking. One can just see him trying out some of its ideas in those living-room dialogues with Taylor or Lowell which friends loved to sit back and listen to as fans enjoy spectator sports. In it he praises what he himself possessed to a high degree: the courage to "read for whim" rather than to follow the trend of the quarterlies, or more popular magazines like *The Saturday Review of Literature* or the *New York Times Book Review Section;* he simply, as Henry James would have applauded him for doing, read and re-read the novels, stories, plays, and poems he personally found interesting.

Jarrell was an advocate of liking works just because one likes them, not because they are famous. These preferences without apology changed reputations: *The Man Who Loved Children* by the Australian novelist Christina Stead, a failure when it appeared in 1940, became a moderate success through Jarrell's article five years later in the *Atlantic Monthly,* a lengthy appraisal reprinted in *The Third Book of Criticism.* It is this sturdiness of judgment for which he pleads in "The Age of Criticism," encouraging all readers to be as nonconformist as the bat-poet. The "age" itself instructs critics thus:

Admit what you can't conceal, that criticism is no more than and no less than the helpful remarks and the thoughtful and disinterested judgement of a reader, a loving and experienced and able reader, but only a reader . . . at your best you make people see what they might never have seen without you; but they must always forget you in what they see. (p. 86)

Where Randall Jarrell is concerned, the last of these injunctions would be unwise to apply. Nobody wants to forget him in the new way of "seeing," nor does his company lessen its joy. Pound's "What thou lov'st well" drove his critic's pen.

Something of that "more" that Jarrell wished for from life he found in teaching, an activity which often seems ephemeral, though it is not so at all: spirit writes on spirit, which in turn continues the process. Randall Jarrell found daily happiness in his daily job. Seymour Krim says: "He chose to work in an obscure girls' college in the South (he was born in Tennessee) rather than in a prestigious university—and he loved teaching above every other activity; he must have been one of America's most effective teachers of poetry."[1] His criticism and translations are interlocked with the classroom; his one novel is set on a campus. Most readers of this present book, very likely, will be either students or teachers. It is for them that it is primarily written, though in a larger sense it is written as Adrienne Rich confessed each of her lyrics to be, for Jarrell himself.

Since "the style is the man," the children's books, like individual poems, give a good picture of their author. So do the critical essays. Though few if any continue to hold the belief that Randall Jarrell is greater as critic than poet,[2] his niche among the giants in criticism is assured. At twenty-five, he was already a rookie in its Major Leagues. In the very first issue of *The Kenyon Review*, edited by John Crowe Ransom, he was publishing analyses of A. E. Housman,[3] his "portrait of the artist as a young man": a result of his attraction to the elegiac Housman born of his own sensibility.

Two of the essays in *Poetry and the Age* are on Robert Frost. Though cognizant of Frost's limitations, Jarrell held him in high honor, an esteem that turned to friendship. Critics have often made difficult poetry clear; Jarrell made Frost's more obscure, even the pieces readers had always taken to be "easy," by pointing out the bleakness at its core.

If his own darker side has sometimes been overemphasized, as by Helen Hagenbüchle in *The Black Goddess*, so has the daylight, common-sense side of Frost, an oversimplification that lessened after *Poetry and the Age* began to gain a place on the textbook shelves of campus bookstores. Out of the list of what Jarrell regarded as Frost's fourteen best poems (how he loved these lists!) some titles ("Fear," "The Pauper Witch of Grafton") are still untaught in university American Literature courses a quarter of a century after the Jarrellian essay "The Other Frost," but others, like "Design," "Directive," and "Provide, Provide" have become frequent choices because Randall Jarrell recommended them.

He was far from unmindful of Frost's weaknesses as person and artist (would the New Englander have been human, lacking these?). The first of the essays on Frost dispraises the later Frost in contrast with the earlier one as having "few of his virtues, most of his vices, and all of his tricks" (p. 31). Again, Jarrell can bring himself to say about the man whose conversational manner in verse had been the prototype for his own: "now that he's old he's sometimes callously and unimaginatively conservative" (p. 38), mentioning in particular Frost's attitude toward atomic war. There is no doubt, however, that Frost was enormously useful to him in working out his own psychological dramas based on the real lives and speech of real men and women. What Wordsworth began, Frost continued.

The second Frost essay, "To the Laodiceans," forgets about faults and sets out to "appreciate." Yet in doing so Jarrell avoids indiscriminate enthusiasm by extolling the poems only for their triumphs of showing "how the world seemed to *one* man" [italics mine] (p. 61). No one realized more fully than he the absence of certain transcendental values from the world of the author of *North of Boston*, nor how different this world was from that wherein Rilke lived, the writer whom of all poets he felt nearest his own Muse. Yet among his American contemporaries, Jarrell could discover no one else who saw so well the humble dailiness that he himself prized as "the stuff of poetry." The mental anguish of ordinary men and women in Jarrell, even though analyzed in an intellectualized way quite opposite Frost's, resembles that of "The Hill Wife," "The Witch of Coös," and others in this genre, which he loved to teach to his Greensboro classes.

*Poetry and the Age* is particularly good on Walt Whitman. Reading what Jarrell says about this poet's coordination of themes through parallelism in syntax shows how much he himself (perhaps unconsciously) owes to the Good Gray Poet. While everyone in this century accedes to the magnitude of Whitman (even Pound in his succinct and affectionate "A Pact"), no one else has really brought him into hearts with quite the humor, wonder, gratitude, and specificity of Randall Jarrell. The chapter on "Mr." Ransom's poetry (Jarrell retained the Mr. throughout life despite their intimacy at Vanderbilt and later Kenyon) makes for enjoyable reading. As elsewhere, "epic catalogs" are featured, twenty of Ransom's poems being singled out for favorable comment (p. 94). The joyous unrestraint of the last paragraph, running into hundreds of words, which compares Ransom's work to a Brueghelian landscape, is typical of critical estimates by this former scholar of Ransom, as is the concluding sentence: no neat little condensation but a breaking off abruptly. This magnificent coda takes the reader by surprise, in that so slender and fastidious a lyricist becomes analogue to the Flemish painter of *Children's Games, The Kermess,* and other scenes teeming with often vulgar human activity.

Much of *Poetry and the Age* consists of reviews done for *Partisan Review, The Nation, The Kenyon Review.* Some of the sections have more appeal than others, such as the piling up of excited adjectives in the introduction to Williams ("the best short criticism ever written on Williams" according to Hyatt H. Waggoner)[4] in contrast to the Wallace Stevens essay, which seems weak and even somewhat prejudiced. Though "Reflections on Wallace Stevens" contains apothegematic sentences ("A good poet is someone who manages, in a lifetime of standing out in thunderstorms, to be struck by lightning five or six times; a dozen or so times and he is great" [p. 134]), it undervalues the later work of Stevens, only recently praised, even as Jarrell himself in "The Obscurity of the Poet" accuses critics of doing to Pope's poetry despite their willingness to grant genius in prose.

Some of the best parts of this first collection are those on Marianne Moore, and on Robert Lowell, of whose *Lord Weary's Castle* he predicts that "as long as men remember English they will read some of the poems in it" (p. 219).

## II  A Sad Heart at the Supermarket

Both title and subtitle ("Essays and Fables") of this volume show the penchant for satiric narration which motivated Jarrell to write *Pictures from an Institution,* though the rollicking repartee is missing from what becomes at times a diatribe. On the dust jacket, Robert Lowell

compares the collection to Matthew Arnold's "Culture and Anarchy."
Both spring from profound dissatisfaction.

This book includes Jarrell's single detailed exegesis of one of his
poems (fourteen pages on "The Woman at the Washington Zoo"),
undertaken only at the urging of his friends "Red" Warren and
Cleanth Brooks, editors of *Understanding Poetry*, where the explication also appears. It begins with the customary deprecation; in Jarrell's
opinion, talking about himself was neither necessary nor to the advantage of the poetry. The lyric was begun soon after he assumed his
Library of Congress consultantship, early in the summer of 1956, when
he was daily driving past the Washington Zoo from his home in Chevy
Chase.

After an apology for attempting something bound to be more untrue
than true, poems ultimately coming out of dreams and wishes that cannot be traced from manuscript sheets (the first draft, as he says, no
longer existing), he identifies his heroine as a distant relation not only
of the lonely women he saw about him in the Library of Congress
reading room or offices but also of those in "The End of the Rainbow,"
"Cinderella," and "Seele in Raum." Already in his forties, he senses an
affinity with her, in whom aging is evident: "I had for her the sympathy of an aging machine part. (If I was also something else, that was
just personal; and she also was something else.)" (p. 161).

Sameness predominates in this character's days: one hundred thousand dresses become one dress which becomes her body, though not in
the sense of making it more attractive. The monotony is reduced to the
diarist's customary "And so to bed." Jarrell tells how he tried, in an
effort to "laminate," to fit in the alphabet of Washington streets, but
unsuccessfully. The Zoo itself stands for the Capital City: it is "a little
Washington" (p. 164). Ever observant, the poet had noted in his morning and evening drives or on Sunday walks with Mary how two or
three stiff white rats really were left untouched in the foxes' unroofed
cage, and how the wolves turned over their horsemeat, glazed by flies,
to the turkey buzzards out of satiety. The organization of the poem
rests on color versus colorlessness, as in the yellow and rose and green
of Pakistan or Indian saris versus the "dull null navy" of the government worker's dress.

Some critics have said that in Shakespeare the future has found
meanings different from those the dramatist intended. It may be that
the vulture is more than man, Jarrell's explanation of it in *A Sad Heart
at the Supermarket*, as he compares the mask it lifts to the costume of

the Frog Prince, removed in that tale's romantic dénouement—a rescue of the woman at the Washington Zoo from her nonlife by a person
of the opposite sex. The vulture is a common symbol for Death, which
will change her, and for which she longs.

Completely unlike this "poemography," from embryonic status to
printed version in the volume named after it, is the first essay in *A Sad
Heart*, "The Intellectual in America." Though reflective of his interests
as the 1960s started,[5] it is not one of Jarrell's better pieces: a berating
of modern society, sometimes with rather shaky allusions, such as the
one to America's Founding Fathers as art patrons (p. 15): Franklin, for
instance, could scarcely be called a devotee of art though he liked a
little fiddle music at the end of his busy day, and even for Jefferson,
art was not a primary concern. Jarrell tries to prevent dating by the
poetic footnote on page 5: "The tide goes in and the tide goes out but
the beach stays sand and the sea stays salt—and it is the sand and the
salt that I am writing about," but the allusions to Presley, Monroe,
Eisenhower, no longer retain their first effectiveness.

In a period when the Department of Health, Education, and Wel-
fare is opposed by state governments that wish to retain an elitist system, wherein teachers are prone to believe that only the body of
knowledge they themselves are conversant with has any importance,
Jarrell's "We are all—so to speak—intellectuals about something" (p.
11)—is refreshing and apropos. Statements like this corroborate the
autobiographical worth of his criticism, a stance upon which Janet
Sharistanian bases her provocative though not entirely convincing
essay on his criticism. She remarks on his use of *tenderness, pity,* and
*affection* in reviews of those authors who awakened enthusiasm in him,
terms which "have very little to do with the concept of the poet as
rebel, seer, or creator of artifacts, but much to do with a definition of
the poet as humanitarian and representative spokesman of his age."[6]

At other times, Jarrell's judgments are simplistic, as when in "The
Taste of the Age" he condemns contemporary versions of the Bible, in
the vein of T. S. Eliot's letters to the *London Times* during the same
period. (His own "Jonah" is a glorification of the King James version,
though it leaves out the whale.) Doubtless he would have come to
realize, with the advance of scriptural research, that a Renaissance version of the sacred text (at least as exclusive of other translations) is no
more desirable than novels, articles, or short stories only in Jacobean
vocabulary and syntax. Were he still alive and of the same view, his
humorous quips would not nullify the present yearning of Jews and

Christians to have the Book of Books available in currently acceptable as well as archaic form.

Many teachers will remember how their interest in the McGuffey readers, called "Appleton" in "The Schools of Yesteryear," was enkindled by that dialogue in *A Sad Heart at the Supermarket*, a lecture by a schoolboy, Alvin, to his grandfather on old-fashioned curricula as against hygiene, home economics, and physical education. The essay reads like an obligato to "A Girl in a Library." There is no attempt at verisimilitude: Alvin does not sound at all like a child, nor his grandfather an old man. They are mouthpieces for Jarrell's annoyance with the pedagogy he saw used around him in North Carolina and by extension elsewhere. The wit is pretty heavy-handed and non-Jarrellian but the thesis is crucial: it is in essence that from first grade on, Blake, Dickinson, Rossetti, Stevenson, Housman, Wylie, to select non-Jarrellian examples at random, should appear in readers or be memorized, rather than the nonentities usually offered, whom none but their mothers have ever heard of. The article falls more under journalism than literary criticism and might better have been omitted, apart from its revival of the McGuffey Reader, a proof that if, as Auden writes, poetry makes nothing happen (a debatable point), prose brings results.

"A Sad Heart at the Supermarket," the title essay, is somewhat smoother ridicule, its butt society for accepting, even seeking mediocrity. Realizing that its carping tone may not be appreciated, Jarrell prepares for rejection in the first paragraph, calling himself "a fool, a suffering, complaining, helplessly non-conforming poet-or-artist-of-a-sort, far off at the obsolescent rear of things, *litotes* meant to amuse"; yet admits that what he has to say "may have a kind of documentary interest" (p. 64). "Medium" seems to replace for him that object of hatred, usury, in Pound, though for less reason. Throughout the book the pronoun *we* expresses a unanimity that no more exists in the real world than does *society* as Jarrell uses it in *A Sad Heart at the Supermarket;* one is always sure Jarrell himself is not a singular "I" within it but its antagonist. Yet no one need be solemn in discussing this hyperbolic tirade, which in any other hands would be far less enjoyable today than it is.

"Poets, Critics, and Readers" is the best of places to unite the three roles Jarrell played so conspicuously well. It contains the famous passage: "I can't imagine a better way [than teaching] for the poet to make his living" (p. 91), a way enjoyable enough to buy as a luxury, were one wealthy. How pleasurable classroom and conference hours could be comes through eloquently in the last piece of *A Sad Heart at the Supermarket*, where he enthusiastically, if with qualifications, reviews *A Wilderness of Ladies*, a book of poetry by his one-time student Eleanor Ross Taylor.

## III   The Third Book of Criticism

Planned by him as a collection shortly before his death, *The Third Book of Criticism* consists of six essays on poetry and three on fiction. (He was never to finish the two other projected ones, on Auden and Chekhov, though the fragments have been well shored against ruin by posthumous publication.) When this third gathering came out in 1969, it was welcome in book form as part of the Jarrell canon. The authors who were the subjects of major treatment (the last chapter skims over poetry between 1910 and 1960) find elucidation in those literary allu sions that give one the sensation of going over with Randall, shelf by shelf, his most precious titles. Christina Stead is not very important of herself, but when the episodes of the Pollits family are interspersed with Proust, Swift, *Faust*, Aristotle, Wordsworth, Conrad, *Moby Dick*, Tolstoy, Shakespeare, Dostoevsky (in addition to all the classics mentioned in the story itself) she seems not only good (as Jarrell calls *The Man Who Loved Children* on page 51) but almost great.

The informality that was an innovation of Jarrell's prevails, in fact is more noticeable than ever, in this posthumous anthology with its questions, contractions, exclamation points, anecdotes. If there is nothing quite so colloquial as the "Peachie keen!" that used to sprinkle Jarrell's talk as remembered by Fanny Cheney, then a Vanderbilt librarian, there is the direct-address *you* and the all-inclusive *we* (really meaning *I* here); opposites tangle and disentangle themselves. The reviewer knows exactly how to alternate quotation and summary to keep attention at a peak. Five or six adjectives accumulate before a noun: "that queer, gypsylike, thin, tanned, pointed face [of Henny] with big black eyes (p. 9)—making the Stead characters so alive that the reader would prefer sharing Jarrell's delight in them to their acting out of their drama in the Stead source.

A reason for Randall Jarrell's extravagant admiration of Christina Stead may be detected in the "criticism as mirror of critic" aspect of the review:

Most of the time she knows that she is better and more intelligent than, different from, the other inhabitants of her world, but the rest of the time she feels the complete despair—the seeming to oneself wrong, *all* wrong, about everything, *everything*—that is the other, dark side of this differentness. (p. 23)

The very title of *The Man Who Loved Children* is descriptive of him: though he never fathered any, he did love children, the affection being warmly returned, as is revealed by a picture in the college annual, *Pine Needles,* where his arms are about two little ones while others gather near, on a flight of stone steps, to listen to a story he is making up for them. Henny bears some resemblance to Jarrell's own mother, Anna, especially in her fainting scenes, and the way she tells her child fairy stories. What he says about Stead could scarcely be more relevant to his own practice: "The commonest and most fundamental principle of organization, in serial arts like music and literature, is simply that of repetition; it organizes their notes or words very much as habit organizes our lives" (p. 39).

If the synopses scattered throughout this essay were deleted, an "Art of Fiction" possibly equal to that of Henry James would remain, starred with comments on the craft, like the parenthetical "One of the most puzzling things about a novel is that 'the way it really was' half the time is, and half the time isn't, the way it ought to be in the novel" (p. 46). What James terms "specificity" becomes in Jarrell "small, live, characteristic, sometimes odd or grotesque details that are at once surprising enough and convincing enough to make the reader feel, 'No, nobody could have made that up'" (p. 27). But James would have eschewed the liberal use of the first person singular, which as this piece of over fifty pages draws to an end more and more replaces the *you* and *we* mentioned above.

In evaluating Stevens's *Complete Poems,*[7] Jarrell gets off to a better start here than in his *Poetry and the Age.* It is true that he seems to be blaming the older writer for not being someone other than himself. Yet when he arrives at the "angelism" which connects those "men of the mind" Rainer Maria Rilke and Wallace Stevens he speaks with the authority of a man thoroughly familiar with a subject, in this case the work of a giant whose importance (despite later objections) he links with that of Hardy, Yeats, and Eliot. Year after year he must have taught the Stevens poems mentioned, and with meticulous preparation. This second chapter gently but significantly phrases reservations about the poet though the total effect is the affirmation of a great talent: "As we read these poems we are so continually aware of Stevens observing, meditating, creating that we feel like saying that the process of creating the poem is the poem" (p. 63).

Jarrell begins his enormous list from Stevens with "The Snow Man," which so many undergraduate Greensboro women must remember with gratitude for all he unveiled to them in this difficult lyric. The two artists had much in common though they were in other ways at variance. An undergraduate of another college, Bess June Moran, reviewing *The Seven-League Crutches* for *The Censer* (The College of St. Teresa, Winona, Minnesota), comments on their likenesses and differences:

Like Wallace Stevens, Jarrell is interested in man's imagination, his "inner self" that is shown by dreams and reveries. But instead of contrasting reality and imagination as Stevens has done, he weaves them together into a theme like that in "A Girl in a Library," in this way portraying life as he believes it to be—a melting pot of reality and fantasy. (Spring, 1952, p. 41)

Jarrell kept several periodicals supplied with the brightest if sometimes sharpest (in a knife-edge sense) analyses of the books that their editors received. His literary journalism constitutes much of this *Third Book*.[8] While treatment here is exemplary rather than inclusive, a stop must be made for his ideas of Robert Graves, whose autobiography, *Good-bye to All That*, he had read at fifteen.

When this critic asks "If you are interested in Graves—and how can anyone help being interested in so good and so queer a writer? . . ." (p. 78), who would have the heart to differ, even the present writer, who feels no such interest? Yet he must have suspected objections, in that the adverb *certainly*, used on the last page, always implies its antithesis: "Graves's poems will certainly seem to the reader, as they seem to me, a great deal more interesting than any explanation of their origin." (p. 112). As with Frost, limitations are not ignored. Yet that Graves was a seminal force in Randall Jarrell is evident from his most direct use in the poems, the archetypal "Woman," that "Mother-Mistress-Muse" who is the White Goddess.

The two long articles on W. H. Auden are introduced by an almost frivolous substitution of that poet's name for the last word in Heraclitus' "We never step twice into the same river." Taken as a unit, the over-seventy pages of this critical biography keep pace with Auden the Pilgrim, walking out of Freudian darkness into Christian light. If not viewing this Pilgrim's movement as Progress, nor ridiculing him for his Anglicanism as Pound did Eliot, Jarrell cannot be expected to approve the transition away from his idol Sigmund Freud even if the replacement be the respected Paul of Tarsus. He condemns with vehemence Auden's failure, in a 1944 *New York Times* review of a Grimm edition, to give cognizance to the horrors of Nazi Germany; to opt in favor of clutching his own "salvation" to his breast rather than concerning himself with European death-camps, with the general holocaust rather than the individual *Angst*.

Jarrell the critic had already included "On Preparing to Read Kipling" in *A Sad Heart at the Supermarket*.[9] Many have wondered at his devotion to Kipling, who is most often thought of as a child's author, a furnisher of heroes for adolescence: that may very well be the reason, tinged with nostalgia, among others, that led the critic to teach, criticize, and edit him so extensively. But this "backward glance" was not all. The reprinted Anchor introduction to *The English in England* begins: "To most of us Kipling means India" (p. 279): in a comparable way, Goethe means Germany and Pushkin Russia. Just as Jarrell read Freud through yearly, so did he *Kim*. Probably some of his colleagues puzzling over *Nightwood* or *The Death of Miss Lonelyhearts* regarded his euologies in print as Pound did the confession of his mother that she enjoyed Marie Corelli: as something he profoundly regretted. The Goddess Fortuna may well put Kipling at the top of the wheel again, changing her mind as she did about Byron.[10] Though Jarrell disclaims in his own instance the desirability of self-references, in *A Sad Heart at the Supermarket* he has gone so deeply into the agonized childhood of Kipling that he might be an analyst, trying to make sense of it. Yet what matters, after all, is the good writing in the stories, and that is where Jarrell's accent falls.

"Fifty Years of American Poetry" was originally the 1962 National Poetry Festival lecture in Washington, D.C., a circumstance affecting Jarrell's style as oral delivery is bound to affect style; later it appeared in the Spring, 1963, *Prairie Schooner*.[11] It repudiates the beatniks (though the need to do so now seems old-fashioned) because of their divorce from the Unconscious, which by the indirection of its images avoids sociology and achieves art. At the same time, it rebukes the moralistic disciples of Yvor Winters, fully as much strangers in the twilight kingdom of Graves's White Goddess despite their reliance on myth for topic. For the major figures—E. A. Robinson, to a lesser degree Edgar Masters and Sandburg, Frost, Pound, Stevens, Williams, Ransom, Eliot,

Moore (whom he tends to overrate in view of his demand that poems rise from that "primitive place," the Unconscious), E. E. Cummings— his judgments are largely positive and usually concurrent with their lasting reputations.

Probably not enough scrutiny has been given to what Randall Jarrell owed Robinson (most of his debt is ordinarily thought to have been incurred to Frost). This realization emerges in the modern-poetry survey: "When you read Edwin Arlington Robinson's poems, you are conscious of a mind looking seriously at a world with people in it and expressing itself primarily in terms of these human beings it has observed and created" (p. 296). Robinson did not entirely "create" his Gardiner, Maine, re-presentations, any more than Jarrell did Nestus Gurley, the actual son of the caretaker on his Greensboro campus, but their mutual need to show understanding in objective form rather than through Shelleyan personal emotion suggests the younger poet as looking to the older one for models.

Conrad Aiken does not fare very well at Jarrell's hands. The author of *The Black Goddess*, Helen Hagenbüchle, even though she realizes the low estimate, comparatively, in which Jarrell held Aiken, sees a likeness between him and Jarrell. After remarking on how Jay Martin, a friend of Aiken's, had written her that Aiken considered Jarrell his enemy, she says in a letter to me: "Whether these feelings of rivalry were mutual I do not know. In any case Jarrell's judgment of Aiken in 'Fifty Years of American Poetry' is not exactly friendly. Nevertheless I have been struck again and again by similarities between the two poets." The connotations of the adjectives Jarrell uses in Aiken's regard are devastating; yet, as if they had been genuinely laudatory, he goes on in the review to speak of Tate in the next paragraph as "Another respected poet."

When he writes "Robert Penn Warren's narrative and dramatic gifts seem to me greater than his lyric gifts . . ." (p. 325) one can only wish him the perspective provided by twenty or more years that we who read Warren now have, so that the view might be changed. About Theodore Roethke, capsule as the ideas are forced to be, he ends with the "right" one, its last aspect canceled by Roethke's death: "Roethke is a forceful, delicate, and original poet whose poetry is still changing" (p. 327).

Robert Lowell was in the habit of sending Jarrell his manuscripts and depended upon the encouragement that he invariably received from his friend. In this omnibus review Lowell is accorded little space but at least is saved till the end, a compliment in itself. Because of his periodic depressions, an interest taking the form of generous praise, made public, was especially valuable: "He is a poet of great originality and power who has, extraordinarily, developed instead of repeating himself. His poems have a wonderful largeness and grandeur, exist on a scale that is unique today" (p. 333). Had Jarrell lived to continue his series of loyal, constructive criticisms, the last poetry and prose of Lowell might have been different.

## IV   Concluding Reflections on Jarrell as Critic

Speaking in the Branford College Common Room at Yale in April 1964, Randall Jarrell told his audience that, unlike some critics who tend to tear apart each book bit by bit, he prefers to assume "the role of a benevolent prophet, trying to find some good in every author's work."[12] Prophet indeed he once was, on the high school *Echoes* staff, but he does not have in mind here its sense of one who foretells the future (he did that too in his educated guesses about the falling-off or increase of reputations); rather, he was gifted with exceptional insight into the realities formed of words placed before him as critic. He resembles the Old Testament prophets who with extraordinary perception saw deeply into the physical environment and moral situations of their day. Benevolent he also was, as a myriad of testimonials to his ethical goodness reveals; in accord with that adjective's etymology, he operated out of good will rather than with the acidity for which he blamed contemporary critics, even though the opposite spirit is frequently a charge against him. Classifying his own age as belonging to the critic rather than, as in the time of Keats to the poet, he decries the preoccupation with minutiae of the New Criticism.

The dominance of the "big-name" quarterlies aggravated this condition which he found so oppressive, a force he came to see more clearly in the 1960s than in the era when Ransom was heading the *Kenyon Review*. Several of these magazines have disappeared, as he expected they would, since in their pages criticism had become an industry rather than an art which first prized and then elucidated. If to know is to love, Jarrell was well qualified to be the sort of ideal critic that any age can use. Ihab Hassam quite justly praises "the very great breadth of his knowledge."[13]

Jarrell had a sophisticated way of concealing whatever disagreeable dicta he felt conscience-bound to make about some of the books sent to him for evaluation, a strategy of taking away with the left hand the pleasant judgments offered with the right, but even more important, derived from the humor he brought to his critical duties. This jocular side wasn't always appreciated: W. D. Snodgrass, who had enrolled, and encouraged Mary von Schrader to enroll, in his Creative Writing Seminar at Boulder, still cannot rise above the hurt feelings occasioned by Jarrell's throwing back his head and laughing uproariously at certain lines of his work: thirty years and more have not removed the humiliation and disheartenment even though he came to look upon the teacher as more influential on his career than any other person.[14] Others were less thin-skinned.

One of the latter was Richard Wilbur. In the 1962 National Poetry Festival address, Jarrell was easier on him than he had been in *Poetry and the Age*, but even so anyone who reads ironically between the lines accorded him will be more impressed by Wilbur's limitations than by his virtues: After some introductory comments on the poet, Jarrell goes ahead to damn his followers without faint praise: "There is another, larger group of poets who, so to speak, come out of Richard Wilbur's overcoat" (p. 329), writers whom he labels as "academic, tea-party, creative-writing-class poets." Wilbur, who read at Old Dominion University in the spring of 1978, wrote me later, "Praising or blaming, he was always so witty that one's final feeling is pleasure in having been an occasion for wit."[15]

It is no wonder that a contemporary who would weather so gracefully the strictures leveled at him in print, recognizing the integrity of the appraiser, probably understood better than most of Randall's associates (excluded here are the chosen few to whom from youth he had opened his heart) Jarrell the man: "As a companion, he never gave the impression that he thought life not quite a fair bargain, quite the contrary; but that is what his poetry says, and I admire him for saying part of the truth so well. Complainers annoy me, but at his best he was always more than that." Though enough vexed by Jarrell's comments on *Ceremony* to challenge the poet-critic, Wilbur regretted his oversensitivity: "I was so stupid as to write him (since we were already friends) a letter of protest. He was very much more positive about me in his third book of criticism, by which I had no doubt changed for the better."[16]

Jarrell, Wilbur feels, also "changed for the better," calling him "an awfully interesting poet to me whose very best work comes in his last book."

Independent ever, Randall Jarrell was at times the voice for a very small minority, as when he wrote negatively of the style of Willa Cather's *Lucy Gayheart,* which most reviewers were lauding.[17] This self-reliance is bracing to encounter. The charm of his floating like a butterfly made less irritating his bee's sting to the stung. Malkoff describes him thus: "As poetry critic of *The Nation, Partisan Review,* and the *Yale Review* at various times, he was respected, feared, and somehow loved in that role."[18]

Respect, fear, and love are all present in Howard Nemerov's thoughts in 1967 about *The Complete Poems* as reprinted in *Reflexions on Poetry & Poetics:*

Randall Jarrell and I reviewed one another amply during his life perhaps as many as three times each; we said, both of us, some harsh things, some funny things, some kindly things, and altogether were nothing if not critical. I should feel sorry to write, from ignoble security, literary criticism that is unable to evoke, indeed provoke, his answering voice[19]

In *The Third Book of Criticism,* with fewer than forty pages of print to cover a half-century of American poetry, Jarrell has time only to wish for room to write about instead of just name Howard Nemerov, whom he calls "interesting and intelligent" (p. 330). Had he lived to read for review *The Collected Poems of Howard Nemerov* (National Book Award winner in 1978), he would have found echoes of himself, the sincerest form, not just of flattery but of the memorability of poems that survive their makers. Jarrell's lyrics taken together have the lastingness of myth, and like myth, they teach; his criticism, so much of it born of delight, has not only taught his fellow-critics to relax from "the scientific approach" into the readability of art but contains in paragraph or sentence, the durable silver and gold of "common speech," prose-poetry such as Nemerov includes in the last section of his own collection. With the fourth volume of commentary on his fellow artists (in preparation), the courage and energy Nemerov credits him with will have gone further toward building the world which he and Nemerov, borrowing from him, feel to be "everything which is the case."[20]

## V    Pictures from an Institution: A Comedy

Jarrell's only novel was rollicking *tour de force,* its title a variant of Moussorgsky's musical composition, itself an improvisation on those views of life painting gives us, as discussed in Chapter 3. Comedy, as in Molière, is always the best way of criticizing human behavior. Contemplated from one angle, the caricature Gertrude is the perfect antithesis of Jarrell the Creative Writing Teacher; if from another, this composite constructor of really very funny barbs has quite a bit in common with the author, possibly more in his private than public talk. The novelist "heroine" is both idolized and feared by the young ladies in a school similar to but not identical with Sarah Lawrence College, where Jarrell taught after coming out of the Army Air Force, just as Gertrude is similar to but different from Mary McCarthy, whose earlier satire of campus life, *The Groves of Academe*, immediately suggests her as candidate for Jarrell's artist-in-residence.

The nineteenth century called Edgar Allan Poe a "hatchet man," and some have felt the same about Randall Jarrell, tending to exaggerate his resemblance to Gertrude. Her specialty in hurting people with her tongue (even though laughter ensues when they seem to deserve it) contrasts with Jarrell's carefulness about the feelings of others in the Women's College in Greensboro, though it may not have been a noticeable trait of his pronouncements at Vanderbilt, Kenyon, even Sarah Lawrence. One of his students, a woman from England now on the Belmont Abbey English Faculty in Belmont, North Carolina, told me how he used to call a girl out of the room into the corridor to say "I am intending to give you *B;* is that all right with you?" Even if the young lady felt she should have had *A*, his consideration brought home the justice of the grade.

Professor Rosenbaum, the hero without quotes, as a good if eccentric teacher, has the humanity Gertrude lacks. Though the narrator is also a professor on this incredible campus, nothing about his pedagogy comes through directly. The antithesis of the "Girl in a Library" is the sensitive, bright Constance, protegée of the Rosenbaums; the students of the "I" must recede before their teacher's fascination with his ferocious woman-colleague: if young poets are no longer wild and woolly but rather "tame and fleecy," as Jarrell told an audience upon taking over his Library of Congress work,[21] Gertrude in her relationship with all but her strangely appreciative husband, Sidney, is about as tame and fleecy as a panther.

Critics of this critique of the stylized finishing school were of many minds about its value as criticism—as they were about the not-as-yet-established critic responsible for it.[22] Opinions on the spirit behind the novel ranged widely. Louis Coxe, saying "Humanly, the book troubles the heart," compared it to "dead life," from the French term for still life *(la vie morte):* these "butterflies," Coxe feels, are definitely impaled.[23] Robert Penn Warren thoroughly enjoyed the comic episodes, recognizing Jarrell's own conversational wit. Francis Steegmuller discerned the Chaucerian compassion concealed under the ironies: "Mr. Jarrell is on the side of the angels." Edmund Fuller, too, introduces angels into his *Saturday Review* capsule comment on *Pictures:* "While it laughs at much of our intellectual pride and pomposity, it also develops a breadth of warm sympathy for the angelic touch that may visit the most foolish of us."[24] Anthony West, who seems to have had no liking for Jarrell the man, sides with Gertrude, both against her creator and his fellow-creations, the Rosenbaums.[25]

Wallace Stevens, that rare exception, a poet who was never a teacher, liked both novel and author. He writes to Bernard Heringman from Hartford on January 29, 1954: "I ran across Jarrell in New Haven a week or two ago when we were both members of the Bollingen committee. He's a delightful fellow and the parts of the novel that have been published seem to me to be of unusual interest and skill."[26] When Knopf sent Stevens a copy for a pre-publication statement, he was cooperative, though such a request went against his usual practice.

Not only for *Pictures from an Institution* but for Jarrell's poetry, too, Stevens had admiration, voting for Jarrell before Richard Eberhart, Delmore Schwartz, and Howard Nemerov in that order when a judge in the competition for the Harriet Monroe Poetry Prize in 1955.[27] Wallace Stevens's poetics, not too unfairly, might be considered as based on "no things but in ideas." Perhaps, since the "supreme" fiction of *Pictures* has ideas rather than characters acting out its travesty of learning, it might have seemed more interesting to him than it has to others who wanted the "I" to be more like the Randall Jarrell they knew, one of the best teachers imaginable. At any rate, this comedy of a novelist appraising a novelist, as if a mirror should talk about another mirror, has attained the status of a work to be savored again and again for its sparkling dialogue, "surgical" as Gertrude's role in it often is.[28]

## VI   A Note on the Translations

The ambition and insincerity of the "system" as caricatured in the novel, light years away from his later North Carolina setting, may give indications of why Jarrell accepted Peter Taylor's invitation to join him in that state. He hated New York, as he used to tell his Greensboro students, and the stint of professorship at Sarah Lawrence belonged to quite another side of the poet than the guide he became to the

Women's College English classes. His desire to win everyone over to the poems he loved is as unlike as possible to the owl-Gertrude's predatory attacks but very close to the bat's efforts with his recalcitrant batkin. The translations, particularly of European lyrics, were inextricable from his efforts to do so.

Anyone who has tried to teach Sophocles and Euripides to undergraduates out of the unnatural, obsolete versions of Victorians, before the advent of Robert Fitzgerald, Richmond Lattimore, David Grene, will agree to the importance of the right words in the right order. Though not knowing Greek any more than Jarrell did Russian, William Butler Yeats has added a standard text of *Oedipus* which surpasses that of the academies in arousing student response. The marked-up classics used in the seminars of "the man who gladly taught" remain as evidence of his attempt to diminish for his students the barriers of space and time.

Among the authors that Jarrell translated, none was more his "double" than Ranier Maria Rilke, mentioned in the first chapter as having the same sense as his own of that sadness possessing the heart of a thinking child. While he never "really" learned German, as "Deutsch durch Freud" insists,[29] he understood it well enough to evaluate the existing renditions and out of them, supported by the original text, to fashion a sheaf of his own, largely posthumously published. Pat Borden, now on *The Charlotte Observer*, re-creates his sharing of these: "One most pleasant memory that stands out is of a rainy late fall day when he read some of Rilke's work at Elliott Hall, our student union. Some thoughtful soul had lit a fire and we sat in clusters around Jarrell's feet on the parquet floor, caught up in the mood."[30]

Preferring Chekhov's *The Three Sisters* above all other dramas and thinking of it daily—Jarrell never stepped twice into the same Chekhov any more than into the same Auden—he aimed at translating it in such a way as to integrate the symbols so carefully into the texture that no "purple passages" would stand out. The result, when acted, brought praise: after a compliment on the avoidance of archaisms, Howard Taubman in the *New York Times* (June 23, 1964) says about the Actor's Studio production: "Mr. Jarrell's version does not draw attention to itself. It is clean, idiomatic, yet timeless." How pleased Jarrell must have been by the reviewer's noting his own affinity to Chekhov: "This translation is a sensitive reflection of Chekhov's art. For one is rarely conscious of lines in themselves." A vertical study of the lengthy notes gathered together, with summaries, in the edition published after his death, gives the key to Jarrellian poetry. What he says about *The Three Sisters* is true about the body of his poems, "so marvelously organized, made, realized, that reading it or seeing it many times to be thoroughly acquainted with it is all one needs" (p. 103).

*The Complete Poems* includes his other translations; the Goethe *Faust*, Part One, has been briefly eulogized in the fourth chapter above. All display him as teacher par excellence, in and beyond the four walls of any classroom. Although a "little homemade rainbow made of tears" sometimes dims the eyes that read Randall Jarrell, the heart taught by him remains a glad and grateful learner.

### CHAPTER 7

# In the Glass of Memory: The Greensboro Graduates Look Back

IF the world is different because of Randall Jarrell, and it is, the reason is that he united seeing and saying, as is logical since "to see" is
related to the Old English verb *secgan,* "to say." By his "saying" he
showed others how to see, as well as to listen, as a full-length study of
music in him, reinforcing and deepening this theme, will one day dem-
onstrate. With the death of this middle-aged "Clerk of Oxford," the
process of remembering began.

When Barbara Lovell read in *The Charlotte Observer* for Friday,
October 15, 1965, the article under the caption RANDALL JARRELL,
TRAFFIC MISHAP VICTIM, she wrote the elegy "Losses," two stanzas of which are used here not only for the pictures they create and
the emotion felt uniquely by this former student but also as a strand in
a general lament:

> The simple protests (it isn't so, it can't
> Be so) do not rise. It is, death
> Is. *A man's look completes itself.*
> And a man's life completes itself . . .
> No, no, for instance, Randall Jarrell,
> My life still failing your courses.

> Is this too strong? Where in the dark
> That those past years are, where is the girl
> In the library? Trying hard to write
> A poem, remembering how, when you lectured,
> You slumped, slant in the chair, and your legs
> Twined round each other like vines.[1]

## I   *Emily Wilson*

Emily Wilson was one of the first alumnae to learn of the accident:

I graduated from Women's College (1961), made a commencement speech
full of allusions to Eliot and Frost, talked with Mr. Jarrell afterwards (in a
white jacket, his arms slipped through the slits in his black robe), and went
out into the world. Four years later late one night the phone rang and a classmate called to tell me she had heard on the late news of the death in Chapel
Hill of Randall Jarrell. I sat on the floor not hearing her voice, but the voice
of my old teacher. Could it possibly be true that his radiant presence was
gone? That the poet I had known was now like all the other poets I had ever
heard of—dead?[2]

It is tempting, since Emily has given leave, to quote verbatim the let-
ter-memoir she wrote on New Year's Day, 1977, prompted by my
inquiry as to her recollections of her teacher. Rather than do so, this
chapter will aim only at a paraphrase, enlivened by quotations. Sum-
marizing her first impressions of Jarrell, she writes: "And when he
appeared in class in his dark beard and tweedy jacket, his bright eyes
holding us in his spell, it was as if all the poets I have ever heard of—
Shakespeare, Keats, Browning—had suddenly been reincarnated in
the person of Randall Jarrell."

Despite his resemblance to Santa Claus (confusing the Greensboro
children), to angels (it is surprising how often people referred to Randall as angelic),[3] and to Prince Charming in the dénouement of "Cinderella," the Poetry Teacher was very human, driving through the
campus in his sports car while Emily and her friends leaned out of
Hinshaw Hall: "There he goes!" It was exciting to watch the superb
tennis player (he who at Boulder in 1951 had offended W. D. Snodgrass, then in his seminar, by telling Snodgrass he was not good enough
to be his partner). The slang terms habitual to Jarrell drifted up to the
girls in the residence hall: "Hadn't I heard him myself as he shouted
'Golly!' and 'Gee Whiz!' in the intensity of his tennis match on the
courts below the dorm?" One day, never to be forgotten, he had even
stopped Emily on the grounds of the Women's College, called her by
name, and made some little remark about her latest poem.

One likes to think of Randall Jarrell as having "a happy heart in the
classroom." Emily describes his joy there as radiant: "He loved to
teach. His voice was such a human voice, heartbreaking or exuberant,

straining with feeling." She remembers his hands, with their long, graceful fingers, which he used to follow the sequence of a line, as in the kinesthetic effect of Hopkins's first verse in "The Windhover." She mentions his special love for "The Snow Man" by Wallace Stevens, "Gerontion" by Eliot, "The Witch of Coös" by Frost. He never gave a sense of rush: "If it took all semester for us to talk about a few poems, we knew them by heart, made them our own." She continues to hear Randall's voice as she reads and teaches the same poems without him.

The students played jokes on him, as on the day when after waiting a long time for his arrival the class left, with a message for him on the blackboard. They had revised one of his favorite places in "The Witch of Coös," when the son-narrator of that ghastly story says, after telling how his father was upstairs and mother downstairs: "I was a baby. I don't know where I was." The explanation ran: "We were in class. We don't know where you were. You was a baby."

At the beginning, the young women rather resented the fact that "their" poet was married, and happily. Emily continues:

Once, after class had started, we heard a tap on the door, and we all looked to see Mary's lovely face in the glass, and she whispered for him to toss her the car keys. When he saw her at the glass, he burst into praise, "Babydoll!" When we invited Mr. Jarrell to read "Cinderella" and some other poems in the parlor of our dorm, Mrs. Jarrell came with him, and they held hands or he stood by her, entwining his arm in the curve of her shawl.

In the end they accepted the wife, flattered by her interest in what they wrote and helped by her comments. Later, they found comfort after the death in that they could still count on keeping in touch with her.

Though Jarrell avoided jobs like committees and the moderating of publications, he was always instrumental in getting, then entertaining, the celebrities who came each year for the *Corradi*'s Arts Festival: Flannery O'Connor, Malcolm Cowley, Grace Hartigan, Louis D. Rubin, Fred Chappell, Elizabeth Hardwick, Robert Lowell, Adrienne Rich, X. J. Kennedy, Karl Shapiro, John Dos Passos, Mark Rothko, Lionel Trilling, R. P. Blackmur. To the students, the most important was Robert Frost, star of the Arts Festival in 1955, 1957, and in other years. About 1960 he appeared in Elliot Hall,[4] to the delight of Emily and the other students:

After the reading Mr. Jarrell invited his writing class to come into the lounge where a table and supper had been set up for Mr. Frost. We sat around him, timid as could be, and asked him questions. Our shy voices must have troubled his old, deaf ears and he would growl at us and ask us to speak up. Mr. Jarrell sat to one side, his hands folded around one knee and watched it all like an indulgent father.

Sylvia Wilkinson, more of whose memories will be given in this chapter, glimpsed during the Frost visit a not altogether amiable poet:

Because of Jarrell, I got to meet Robert Frost. I remember looking at the old man, his face covered with age spots that looked like freckles when he was laughing—we discussed a walking cane that Jarrell had, whether the head was a dog or a mule, and how it was formed into a twisted shape because a vine strangled the stick it was made from when the stick was trying to grow. Also during that meeting I saw a bitterness in Frost I was unaware of, and an incredible sensitivity to criticism that made him angry even when the criticism was unfounded or unintended.[5]

When Emily Wilson (now Emily Wilson Herring) saw the facsimile of "A Girl in a Library," featured in *Pine Needles* with a full-page photograph of a student whom Emily calls "one of us," sitting with shoes on and open eyes, a book on her lap, in the Walter Clinton Jackson Library, the effect was epiphanic: "When I saw that picture and read the poem and knew the poet, art and life came together for the first time." Since then, book by book, she has built a complete collection of Jarrell first editions, the last a 1977 Christmas gift of *The Seven-League Crutches*, the first collection in which "A Girl in a Library" was published. Feeling that she and her fellow-students "was too few," she asks: "When the place of Randall Jarrell is fixed in literary history, will there be enough of us to tell how he was alive?"

## II  *Heather Ross*

Heather Ross Miller, niece of Mrs. Peter Taylor, and classmate of Emily Wilson in the Commencement of 1961, is another grateful student who intends to keep trying to tell how Randall was, alive:

I have been collecting thoughts and writing down memories of Randall ever since his death in 1965. I hope to get them all finished this summer [1978] for eventual publication in a book of essays I call *Children, Gods, and Men*—and you KNOW where that title comes from!

I call the section on Randall "The White Snake," from an old, old Grimm tale, another archetype, no doubt, with parallels to Solomon's wisdom and his ability to talk to birds and animals. The snake kissed Solomon's ears and he was then blessed with these powers. Randall was like that, to me at any rate. Blessed with powers to interpret, to see the truth, to know.[6]

About the 1961 Jarrell reading, Heather elaborates in her second letter: "I so clearly remember his pink shirt, his beard, his overwhelmingly warm rapport with the Pfeiffer College students—so many of the students came up to him afterward and told him that hearing him read his own poems was exactly like having a religious experience." Over fifteen years after this event, to her enormous joy, she discovered in a Caedmon catalog "OH, WONDER OF ALL WONDERS—Randall Jarrell reading and discussing his poems against war—this last one [the other two were recordings of *The Bat-Poet* and *The Gingerbread Rabbit*] made at Pfeiffer College in 1961." She goes on to explain: "What a lucky quirk of fate—somebody just happened to turn on a tiny little tape recorder that afternoon—and here we have a record reproduced by Caedmon."[7]

Heather Ross Miller vehemently denies the charge sometimes leveled against Jarrell, that his poetry is sentimental: " . . . surely the most despised of all emotions, especially where Randall Jarrell was concerned. How we hated soap-opera sentiment, after sitting in his classes at WCUNC, after hearing him read with such clear and exact emotion." After the ridicule of Shelley's "Indian Serenade" by the New Critics, it has taken poetry a long time to dare to be open and vulnerable, emotionally, but the disciple of Ransom had absorbed certain ways of avoiding sentimentality and developed his own.

### III   *Barbara Lovell*

Barbara Lovell, lines from whose elegy "Losses" are cited above, antedates by a decade Emily and Heather, but her impressions are fully as lasting:

In 1951, when I was eighteen or nineteen at the most, one of the student literati, associated with *Coraddi* I believe, sought me out and said, "Randall

Jarrell wants to see you." I was astonished, apprehensive, and chiefly bewildered. I'm not sure, green, new thing that I was, I'd ever *seen* him though certainly I knew of his existence. The way one knows of God's. As it turned out, he had somehow come across a slight verse of mine published in a little campus anthology of freshman work. What he had to say to me was that he saw merit in it. As a matter of fact, what he said was that I was one of two students (please remember this was in the very early fifties and many far finer writers than I passed through his presence after those days) that he'd encountered that he thought—I'm not certain of his exact phrasing here, but the sense was—really "had it." (The other student, I'm fairly certain, must have been Jean Farley).[8]

Not until the 1970s did Barbara begin to publish—a dozen or so poems and some fiction—but it is Jarrell she credits for the career she feels to be opening out: ". . . he struck the match and the fire never quite went out."

One can visualize Jarrell's life as a teacher in his thirties from the specific details kept safe by his freshman admirer: the long corridor-like office in the basement of McIver building (no longer there) which he shared with Mackie, his desk the window one, where he practiced the acme of communication—to be honest and kind at the same time. It was the year before he went away to Washington for the Library of Congress Consultantship. Deprived of his help, Barbara substituted by memorizing lines of *Little Friend, Little Friend,* and *Blood for a Stranger,* also *Losses,* and handing in writing to the colleagues whom he left behind, but she missed the many sunny afternoons in his office talking books, "books he loved, books I *must* read *right then* if I were ever going to make a poet." Her most cherished possession is the list of over a hundred that grew out of these chats, wherein the handwriting of Jarrell showed the fervor of his recommendations, showed "his passion for the books and his odd but absolutely right sense of selection for the illiterate that I was.[9] What I wish is that I could reproduce his pell-mell commentary on the books as he wrote. It was so compelling that though I have read fewer than I have not read, I have a love—the contagion from his love—just for the titles."

As a senior and editor of the *Coraddi,* she found him kind, but their lives did not mesh as before in that "magical year" (as she calls it) when she was first inspired by the teacher who "was incredibly generous with his time, his knowledge, his enthusiasms." That teacher survives in her own classes at UCNC Charlotte:

It angers me that "Death of the Ball Turret Gunner" is almost the only thing anthologized, though I do teach one text that includes the Donatello David poem. I *wish* they'd include what *I* think are among his finest: "A Girl in a Library," "The Knight, Death, and the Devil," and above all, the very beautiful "Nestus Gurley."

Shortly before Jarrell's death, Barbara Lovell read a newspaper feature on his and Mary's life, including their bird-watching, which prompted her to write him "to thank him for past kindnesses, and to ask if he were aware that a certain Nestus Gurley had been maintenance superintendent or some such when we had been at the Women's College in the fifties. He never answered." How much the poem "Nestus Gurley" means to her is evident from the first stanzas of her "Losses":

> It was not the *Sun*, the *Star* or the *Times*
> That brought the word. Your face leaped
> To me from a page, second front, of the *Observer*
> And I observe, yes, that an accident killed
> And the sun was not darkened, the stars
> Did not fall.
>
> Ah, Randall Jarrell,
> What has happened that this news
> Came not with a dawn where horses
> Stamp in Grecian grasses and the soul salutes
> *With a note or two that with a note or two*
> *Would be a song?*

When the poet, long ago, had gone away from Greensboro for the Library of Congress appointment, he had "very strongly invited" her to write him of her reading and send her poems, which he promised to criticize, but she was much too shy, submitting the lyrics instead to Peter Taylor, who returned them with such comments on the back as "imitation R. J. but pretty good imitation." In relation to this missed opportunity she says, "[I] am now ashamed of myself for that."

## IV  *Sylvia Wilkinson*

Sylvia Wilkinson is another former student (probably the most famous in fiction) who keeps trying to say in prose and in lectures at creative writing seminars how Jarrell was alive. To her, he was not the critic of literature people talked about after his death: "I realized I knew nothing of that. He was my teacher and I wanted to write as much as I could because he was so thrilled when I showed it to him."[10]

At twenty, Sylvia had signed up for his class, her admission due to age rather than ability, as she was too old for Robert Watson's advanced composition class. Speaking at William and Mary College in the spring of 1979, she tells how she emerged from the anonymity in which she had been writing since she was twelve:

I gave him a story which he read in class, anonymous, to protect us (a luxury I don't allow my students). He got to a word, "dompass," and stopped, asking the class if anyone knew what a dompass was. The child in the story was trying to get a dompass from a bubble gum machine. At this point I raised my sweaty palm and said, "Mr. Jarrell, it's supposed to be a compass." From that moment on I became a public writer.

Because of his expressive reading voice he made their stories sound much better than they really were. She took every course he taught and never cut a single class (21 hours of Jarrell): "He loved to read to us, Peter Taylor stories, German fairy tales he had translated, Rilke poems. Sometimes, his wife, Mary, would be there when he read and would sit in a semi-circle with us. They both wore beautiful, dramatic clothes, in a time when people were bogged down in drab, conservative styles. Mary wore panchos [sic] and heavy wools and velvet, Mr. Jarrell wore plain suits in autumn colors."

After evoking from the past the Jarrell family's Christmas wreath of nuts and cones, in "the little house in the woods," together with Betty Watson's giant oil portrait of Randall now in the University of North Carolina–Greensboro library, and cats that seemed large as if in a jungle (an impression possibly due to her own ninety pounds), she admits: "I guess my memories of him are mostly personal, little things. I was totally unaware of how important he was to me—the day he called me to his office and told me, 'Miss Wilkinson, you have a gift' will always be one of the high points of my life. But my reaction, I swung around light poles all the way back to my dorm room, was so young." She finishes assessing his impact on her thus:

He was a man who had powerful reactions. Nothing passed him casually. He could be powerfully sad and powerfully happy. Sometimes I was sorry I had told him of my sorrows because I made him hurt worse than I hurt. He was a truly inspired teacher. A semester of poetry was the intense study of one long poem: "The Lovesong of J. Alfred Prufrock" for English poetry, "Home Burial" for American. Out of it came a method that would stay with all of us.

## V    *Pat Borden and Frances Lomax*

Also out of the 1950s come the recollections of Pat Borden, referred to earlier in regard to Jarrell and Rilke: "Sylvia's accounts of his courses inspired me to take Writing Workshop the first semester of my senior year. I turned in a couple poems and a few short stories and went to hear Jarrell read poetry on various occasions".[11] He was a little stooped and seemed frail when he wore his tweedy jackets with the patch sleeves. He always seemed a little rumpled and shy. Except when he read poetry. He was excellent. I wish—oh, how I wish!—I'd tape recorded some of his readings. Every syllable got its due, complete with facial expressions and body language."

With anyone of strong character, especially when some aspects of it are minority reports (no smoking and drinking, dislike of parties and gossip), opinion is bound to be mixed, and so it was on the campus. Pat gives the positive and negative estimates, concluding with her own: "There were his devotees, like Sylvia, and there were his detractors, the more cynical students who mistrusted his saintly aura. They muttered things about his having a Jesus complex, suspecting that he put on the appearance of extreme gentleness and kindness. But I can't imagine faking the warmth that his brown eyes radiated."

In that same period Frances Lomax (now Ross), who graduated in 1951, took two courses under "Dr. Jarrell's gentle guidance," courses wherein he loved to read to the students and to listen attentively to their interpretations. One day the seminar "collaborated" with him on "a class poem which he neatly wrote on the blackboard, the subject a changing neighborhood." She "always marveled at his simple genius, the adjective inspired by his assumption that everyone was as smart as he" (letter to the author, June 25, 1979).

Mrs. Ross concludes her specific memories: "One cold winter afternoon in another class we found ourselves in the basement (I think) of the very old McIver Building, where he had his office. The class consisted of just a few members and in deference to the temperature, we gathered there. He noticed my shivering and took his tweed jacket and insisted that I drape it around me. To this very day I feel warmed by the magic of that old coat and the greatness of the man who wore it."

## VI  *Bertha Harris and Others*

Bertha Harris, who became a novelist, feels that her point of view, exercised in retrospect, is limited: "I was Jarrell's student for only a year—it seemed longer, since I was doused with the legend before he arrived and certainly knew what I was missing after he was gone."[12] The first of her family to go to college, she had had what she describes as a "deprived childhood"—"meaning no money; no inherited sense of culture or its uses. Whatever aesthetic sense I had was a jumble of addictive and eclectic reading, church ritual, and the Saturday afternoon broadcasts from the Metropolitan Opera." Somehow this preparation for the one Jarrell class she took sounds considerably better than what the prototypes of "A Girl in a Library" had.

To Bertha, whose feelings after twenty years are "as complicated as they are dim," meeting Jarrell was a great event:

Randall Jarrell was the first real, the first "true-to-life" *artist* I ever came up against. . . . There were other artists in residence at the time. Robert Watson is one of them. But Jarrell, because he was employed to be "artist" first, teacher second, had a special impact. Because of his unique position in the English department and in the college at large, he was a compound of all the elements that could not fail to have an impact on the mad, wild greedy young woman I was; he was famous (they told us); he was legend, myth; his gift elevated him up and beyond usual human circumstances; he was a "successful" artist. People wrote about him and listened to him and gossiped about him. People protected him and rewarded him. Other famous poets and writers visited the campus because of him.

Later, she would find out the "real world" is quite unlike its microcosm, a small women's college in the South. She concludes her reminiscences with "I love so much of his work and his image, still: nothing in American letters will ever touch 'The Woman at the Washington Zoo.'"

Dure Jo Gillikan, also of the 1950s, kept on studying her "new master" after his death until she was able not only to compile a bibliography on him (1941–1970) for the New York City Public Library but to preface it with a three-page "appreciation," which will probably reach more readers than the Greensboro tributes. In introducing the references, Dure Jo calls Jarrell "a man of great humanity and dazzling wit"; she praises *Poetry and the Age* as bringing poetry back from the "cold light of the scholars' microscope . . . into the sun." Her bibliography includes the years covered by Margaret Kissingler's for 1958–1965, but even were the two nothing but repetitive hers would be valuable for the submerged memories out of which it grows. One of her most unusual insights is in associating Jarrell himself with the mockingbird in *The Bat-Poet;* she calls it the Jarrell of birds, solely on its persistent effort to distinguish the real from the unreal. She describes him as writing about a quartet: soldiers, women, children, and animals, powerless subjects who appear and reappear throughout the six volumes to come out before his death. When the *Greensboro Daily News* for March 2, 1966, printed tributes to Jarrell, it included her elegy, influenced by Hart Crane but even more by her genuine affection·

> The moon rises, a smiling Jack-o-lantern,
> Ringed with a halo of bright, winking stars
> That swarm about the sky in great confusion.
> (One of them has a beard and is quite witty)
> As the whining comet sings across the night
> Into the waiting and unfolding sun.
> The wind, now playing the October leaves,
> Sounds almost like laughter.
> He is dreaming now—
> A greater dream.

She is pictured with him, together with Alma Graham, at the student party in his honor when he left for the Library of Congress.

Alma, in this issue, remembers that "when he smiled and his teeth gleamed through his beard, he looked like a mischievous rabbit who'd been up to something" (perhaps to running away from a "kitchen" into the wild wood where the images of his lyrics hid). This picture complements the spellbinder at the evening poetry readings. Alma, from Raleigh, North Carolina, recalls of his religious beliefs: "Mr. Jarrell's reverence for God was real, and went deep. What he hated was the shallow thinking that led to meaningless abstractions and clichés."

The spring after his death, the three alumnae Bertha Harris, Jo Gillikin, Alma Graham, with a fourth, June Cope Bencivenni, as is described in this issue of the *Greensboro Daily News,* began raising funds for The Randall Jarrell Creative Writing Scholarship, so that each year a young writer of marked ability could study at UNCG

Greensboro. The scholarship idea caught on, its resources swelled by royalties from the Lowell-Taylor-Warren memorial volume. In 1977–78 the Jarrell Scholar was Jim Clark, who had come from editing the *Vanderbilt Poetry Review* in Nashville. Born in Cookeville, Tennessee, he had been directed from Tennessee Technical University by one of its professors, George King, who had been at Vanderbilt when Davidson was teaching there; King saw promise in this freshman who was already composing verse influenced by W. S. Merwin and Jarrell.[13]

Jim Clark's "A Letter: After All This Time" prefaces this book: it was written on the twelfth anniversary of the subject's death, a more fitting gift than the anonymous bouquet of artificial flowers on the grave that day in the Guilford cemetery. Now the author of the unpublished *Dancing on Canaan's Ruins*, Jim writes: "What I originally liked, and continue to like, about Jarrell as a poet, is his ear for the lyric—for music." The music and the "music" of Randall Jarrell live on.

# *Epilogue*

### Letter to a Ghost: Randall Jarrell

Once you were script on the margin of a poem,
An iamb that the students made trochee,
A face (smiling or sober) in some reference work.
Today, on my shelf, you are neighbored by Red Warren,
Bob Watson, friends such as I never came to be.
I wonder what would have happened had we met.
Greensboro now is the house set back from the road
Where the stone rabbit runs from the new pool.
Your room has become guest quarters, not for a ghost
But for scholar after scholar, come from afar.
Sometimes you race up the grass with the paperboy
Seeing how far you can throw the *Morning Star*.
It is not true to say we were strangers, Randall,
And death is no fence, but a bridge to where you are.

# Notes and References

### Chapter One

1. This analogy, which prevails almost as strongly as metamorphosis, is explored in respect to Jarrell's poetry in my essay "Randall Jarrell: Landscapes of Life and LIFE," *Shenandoah*, Summer, 1969, pp. 49–78.

2. Introducing his section of first poems in the Ciardi-edited *Five Young American Poets* (New York, New Directions, 1940), Jarrell was explicit on the point: "I don't want the poems mixed up with my life or opinions or picture or any other regrettable concomitants" (p. 40).

3. First Supplement. New York, H. W. Wilson and Co., 1963, p. 487. *Who's Who* for 1963 also implies the 1952 marriage to Mary von Schrader to be his only one.

4. "I'm coming apace with the letters. Becoming discriminating—at last—and finding a pleasant rhythm of episodes in RJ's life that the letters build toward and subside from" (letter to the author May 6, 1979).

5. The 1915 Nashville directory lists Owen, then a bookkeeper, and Anna as living at 2202 Grantland Avenue; by 1920 only Anna C. is named, then residing at 1501 Linden Avenue; in 1926 both parents were living at 6 Evelyn Court, whereas two years later only Anna's name appears at this address.

6. *Randall Jarrell 1914–1965* (New York, Farrar, Straus & Giroux, 1967). Anna Jarrell gave a pictorial record of her elder son's childhood to Suzanne Ferguson for *The Poetry of Randall Jarrell* (Baton Rouge, Louisiana State University Press, 1971), which includes one snapshot of Randall at fourteen with the face of an angel; like Shelley, he was frequently likened to angels by reminiscing friends.

7. Sister Bernetta Quinn, "Jarrell's Desert of the Heart," *Analects*, Spring, 1961, p. 25.

8. Interviews with Mrs. Albert Ganier (Bitsy) of Nashville, March 17, 1979, and January 8, 1980.

9. Bitsy went to school with Mary Davidson, daughter of Randall's thesis director, and later ran a successful farm near Nashville. According to Bitsy, he preferred playing with Betty Friedland, whose father translated the Parthenon from plastic models to a permanent material. Whenever Randall and Betty were faced with a competition, however, he would back away, not wanting the pressure of a tournament.

10. Interview with Lucie, now Mrs. Albert Kay of Falls Church, Virginia,

May 5, 1979. Though she is invalided with multiple sclerosis, her memories of Randall are clear, and she owns two of his paintings (ballerinas).

11. Especially by Lawrence Karl Noriega, who has based his unpublished doctoral dissertation for the University of Virginia (1973) upon it: "The Wisdom That Is Pain: Disillusion as Form in the Poetry of Randall Jarrell" (DAI, 34, 4276A).

12. An expansion of biographical data re this period can be found in "The Group of Two" by Mary Jarrell, the first version of which appeared in *Harper's Magazine*, April 1967, pp. 63–80, together with a photograph and the poem "A Man Meets a Woman in the Street."

13. It was the end of what he recalls in "The Lost World," which Donald Stauffer in *A Short History of American Poetry* (New York, Dutton, 1974), p. 371, reads as "his strange, half-real, half-make-believe boyhood years in Hollywood. Stauffer apparently thinks that "Pop" was Randall's father.

14. Charles, who eventually went to Paris, where he still lives, returned for both Randall's and their mother's funerals.

15. A 1931 *Echoes* calls Randall distinguished for his white tennis shoes.

16. *Yale Daily News*, April 16, 1964.

17. Letter to author April 21, 1979. Though Bissinger, several years older, regarded Jarrell as basically a loner, he mentions one friend, Bert Bacherig (later a television script writer under the name of Peter Barry and now dead), who objected to being awakened in the middle of the night at the Jarrells by Randall's climbing through the porch window to get him to go walking along Nashville's deserted streets.

18. *Echoes*, November, 1929, pp. 9–10.

19. Ibid., March, 1930, pp. 16.

20. This Shakespearean tragedy was to take on painful personal meanings for Jarrell, who remarks on the University of Wisconsin Tape 2134 that Hamlet was "dead right" in his view of re-marriage.

21. In the spring of 1931 Jarrell also acted in Owen Davis's *The Nervous Wreck*, co-starring with Dorothy Moody. In the winter of 1929 he directed a successful *Ten Nights in a Barroom*, together with Virgil Francis. His cousin Bitsy, a Peabody girl rather than Hume-Fogg student, remembers seeing him play a detective on another occasion.

22. The Hume-Fogg graduate Bernard R. Breyer refers to this class prophecy as "cruelly hilarious," though now that for the world at large the barbs cannot be detected, one can only surmise its importance as a rehearsal for *Pictures* (letter to author, June 13, 1979).

23. Breyer, now on faculty of Alabama Polytechnic Institute in Auburn, writes the author on May 5, 1979: "From time to time I have thought it would be an act of piety to set down my remembrances of Randall, for they are, many of them, very dear and droll. But on the other hand I have long inveighed against biography as more injurious to the interpretation of literature than helpful." Breyer and Randall must have shared a friendship of

some depth in their boyhood, judging from the former's contribution to the *Essays in Honor of Walter Clyde Curry* (Nashville, Tennessee: Vanderbilt University Press, 1964): "A New Look at *Julius Caesar*," pp. 161–181.

24. In an interview with Rose Breyer Martin March 16, 1979 (another sister who went on to Vanderbilt, in economics) I learned much about Randall's relationship with her family, and was shown his Degas-like painting and a snapshot of him at the beach with his friends, the Milton K. Starrs, who used to take Randall South with them, as well as to Cape Cod. Jarrell dedicated *Little Friend, Little Friend* to Sara Starr, and a lyric, "The Head of Wisdom," to Katherine Louise Lyle Starr.

25. *Echoes*, November, 1930, p. 20.

26. Letter to author April 11, 1979.

27. Letters to Randall from Amy, written in 1942–43, are preserved in the Berg Collection of the New York Public Library. Several of his to her during the army years are owned by Lucie Breyer Kay, Falls Church, Virginia.

28. Interview with Rose Martin March 18, 1979. Mrs. Martin relates how Randall in uniform appeared one night while on furlough to visit their mother, Mrs. Breyer; she being out, he spent the evening conversing with Rose.

29. Mackie Jarrell in a May 28, 1979, letter to author remembers that Randall often spoke of Amy and of her family: "I knew certainly that he had loved her long and deeply."

30. His comment cited in *Time*, September 15, 1967.

31. This was the year that his future wife, Mackie Langham, was awarded a Master's degree in English at the University of Texas, Austin. She plans to write her own memoirs of Randall some day (letter to author August 24, 1978).

32. Xeroxed copy of this letter sent to author by Mrs. Ferguson: "He was inclined to talk a great deal in class. There was nothing shy or withdrawing about him."

33. See especially Mary Jarrell's article.

34. May 14, 1979.

35. In Radcliffe Squire's *Allen Tate and His Work*, University of Minnesota Press, (Minneapolis, Minn., 1972), Lowell describes his first arrival at the Tates' in "last summer's mothballish, already soiled white linens, and mocassins," and his second, when he solved the problem of too many house guests (Ford Madox Ford and his secretary were staying there) by taking the Tates literally and buying a Sears Roebuck tent (pp. 34–35).

36. Robert Lowell, *Selected Poems* (New York, Farrer, Straus, Giroux, 1976), pp. 171–72.

37. *Writers at Work Second Series* (New York, Viking, 1963), p. 368.

38. Interview, March 16, 1979.

39. In 1973 Martin Seymour-Smith in Funk & Wagnall's *Guide to Modern World Literature* gives three pages to Jarrell and quotes from four of his

poems (New York, 1973), pp. 163–65: "It has been given to few American poets to write so beautifully and so simply—and to avoid the psychopathic, the abnormal, the terrible, at the same time" (p. 165). MacDowell, however, still thinks Randall's assertion unwarranted.

40. Elena Wilson (ed.), *Letters on Literature and Politics 1912–1972* (New York, Farrar, Straus & Giroux, 1977), pp. 362 and 370.

41. *Kenyon Review*, III, p. 379.

42. *The Poetry of Randall Jarrell*, p. 3.

43. *The Habit of Being*. Letters edited and with an introduction by Sally Fitzgerald (New York, Farrar, Straus, Giroux, 1979), pp. 54, 74, 71.

44. Brochure of the Jackpine Press, Winston-Salem, North Carolina.

45. The same photograph is used on the dust jackets of *The Complete Poems* and *The Third Book of Criticism*.

46. "Go, Man, Go," *Mademoiselle*, May, 1957, p. 98.

47. A University of Wisconsin Tape 2134.

48. Mr. Ragan and his wife edit that remarkable weekly *The Southern Pilot*, Southern Pines, North Carolina.

49. Howell Campbell, Jr., remembers Anna as a cultivated, loving, intelligent woman, a great help to him in raising his own children (telephone conversation with author May, 1979).

50. *The New York Times*, November 9, 1965, reports that Dr. Louis G. McKinney, acting medical examiner who signed the death certificate, said that a three-week investigation surrounding Mr. Jarrell's death had "raised a reasonable doubt about its being suicide" (p. 19).

51. Jarrell's "Answers to Questions" in *Mid-Century American Poets*, John Ciardi, ed. (New York, New Directions, 1950), p. 182.

## Chapter Two

1. "Randall Jarrell," In *The Modern Poet*, ed. Ian Hamilton (New York, Horizon Press, 1969), p. 155.

2. The Gordian Press (Staten Island, New York, 1966), pp. 168–207.

3. "The Dramatic Lyrism of Randall Jarrell," *Poetry* 79 (March, 1952), 338.

4. The five questions after "Burning the Letters" in *An Approach to Literature*, Cleanth Brooks, John Purser, and Robert Penn Warren, eds. (New York, Appleton-Century Crofts, Inc. 1939) throw light on this early lyric, especially the fifth: "In her head (see 1. 1) he has hitherto had a country in which he has not changed. Now he still has a 'home' there, but a burial place merely—not a place in which to live unchanged, but a place in which his dead body, his death now accepted, can rest" (p. 367). This text has molded thousands of student-responses.

5. "Randall Jarrell: A Stand-In's View," *Southern Review* 9 (Autumn,

1973), 883. Jarrell himself tended to prefer "Eighth Air Force," feeling that it better expressed his reaction to the war than any other poem he ever wrote. Cited in *Poet's Choice,* Paul Engle and Joseph Langland, eds. (New York, Dial Press, 1962), p. 140.

6. "The Wisdom That Is Pain: Disillusion as Form in the Poetry of Randall Jarrell," (DAI 34:4276A 1973,) referred to in Chapter 1. Noriega, who greatly admires "Eighth Air Force," would probably include it as one of Jarrell's clarifications of reality: "In the manner of his necessary angels, Frost, Stevens, and Rilke, Jarrell created figments of language in order to make his audiences see through the spurious and unconscious figments of life."

7. Jarrell's footnote in *Selected Poems* reads: "The man who lies counting missions has one to go before being sent home."

8. Cf. James L. Jackson's note on it in the April, 1961, *Explicator.*

9. "An Affable Misery: On Randall Jarrell." *Encounter* 39 (October, 1972), 46. It is even included in Record 2485 done by Ruby Dee, etc. on mostly black writers, *Tough Poems for Tough People,* in the collection of audiovisual materials at the University of Wisconsin, Madison. Explanatory notes on it abound, including P. J. Horman's "Jarrell's 'The Death of the Ball Turret Gunner'," *Explicator,* Summer, 1978, pp. 9–10; P. F. Bassett's note in the Spring, 1978, *Explicator,* pp. 20–21; and David K. Cornelius's in the previous volume of that magazine, Autumn, p. 3.

10. Few critics have better expressed the dreadfulness of "The Death of the Ball Turret Gunner" than George Greene in "Four Campus Poets": "An inferno quality vibrates here appallingly: the anonymous youth curled in pathetic imitation of the womb, his bloody fur freezing in arctic air six miles above the earth, a limp mass to be removed as one might wash away spilt gasoline" (*Thought,* Summer, 1960, p. 235).

11. Nitchie, "Randall Jarrell: A Stand-In's View," p. 888. See note 5 above.

12. November, 1954, p. 94.

13. One aspect of the complexity was the war as expressive of what in Robert Penn Warren would have been named Original Sin, and in Karl Malkoff is enunciated in terms recalling the Noriega note above: "What is finally most significant about Jarrell's war poems is that they encounter war not as a perversion of this human condition, but, unfortunately, a clarification," *Crowell's Handbook of Contemporary American Poetry* (New York: Thomas Y. Crowell Company, 1973), p. 149.

*Chapter Three*

1. In our correspondence I had urged Jarrell to include "Giselle" and another lyric in a collection: when he sent me the inscribed *The Woman at the Washington Zoo,* he wrote on the fly-leaf "To Sister Bernetta, with much

gratitude, from Randall Jarrell. As you see, I've put in *Giselle* and *A Ghost, a Real Ghost.*"

2. "Randall Jarrell: The Integrity of His Poetry," *Centennial Review* 17 (Summer, 1973), 237.

3. He reviewed Walter McElroy's translation of Corbière in the *New York Times Book Review* September 28, 1947.

4. *An Introduction to the French Poets: Villon to the Present Day* (London: Methuen 1973) p. 233.

5. *Hypnotism* (New York, E. P. Dutton, 1927), p. 25. Jarrell repeats this scene in the autobiographical "The Child of Courts": "I hear him breathing slowly, as he bends/ Above me" (*Losses*, p. 45).

6. L. W. Lawrence, *Hypnotism* (Chicago, The Henneberry Company, 1901), p. 35.

7. *The Achievement of Randall Jarrell A Comprehensive Selection, with a Critical Introduction* (Glenview, Ill.: Scott, Foresman, 1970), p. 1.

8. *French Literature: Its History and Meaning* (Englewood Cliffs, N.J., Prentice-Hall, 1973), p. 204.

9. Both the alternative translation of "Afterwards" and the comments on it in C. F. MacIntyre's *Tristan Corbière Selections from Les Amours Jaunes* (pp. 234–238) are most pertinent to further study of how "Lady Bates" is grounded in the *rondels* imagery. Berkeley and Los Angeles, University of California Press, 1954, 67–85.

10. *Greensboro News*, October 16, 1965. The assistant city editor, Lane Kerr, shows unusual understanding of Jarrell in his "He Never Talked of Himself."

11. Hoffman, *The Achievement of Randall Jarrell*, p. 17. "Just being in Nashville upsets me," Randall writes Amy in an undated letter of the Army period.

12. *Randall Jarrell* (Minneapolis, Minn. University of Minnesota Press, 1971), p. 30. Rosenthal is better on "Lady Bates" in *The Modern Poets*, saying that, as in "A Girl," Jarrell is trying to evoke "an acute sense of violated sensibility" (p. 246). In *The Modern Poets* he comments favorably on "A Girl in a Library," even though his interpretation does not seem particularly Jarrellian: "His satire is tempered by compassion for her as an innocent victim of her times who might at least, in another age, have been one of the anonymous 'braided maidens singing as they spin'" (New York, Oxford University Press, 1960), p. 9.

13. Rosenthal, *Randall Jarrell.*

14. *Randall Jarrell 1914–1965*, p. 116.

15. Noted by George Hemphill in "The Meters of the Intermediate Poets," *Kenyon Review* 19 (Winter, 1957), 45.

16. *Partisan Review* 22 (Fall, 1955), 496–513.

17. *Pushkin Threefold*. (New York, Dutton, 1972), p. 435.

18. Cf. my article "Warren and Jarrell: The Remembered Child," *Southern Literary Journal* 8 (Spring, 1976), 24–40.

## Chapter Four

1. Donald Barlow Stauffer, *A Short History of American Poetry* (New York, Dutton, 1974), p. 36.
2. *The Sculpture of Donatello* (Princeton, New Jersey, Princeton University Press, 1963), p. 83.
3. *Randall Jarrell 1914–1965*, p. 111.
4. Louis Becherucci in *The Encyclopedia of World Art* (New York, McGraw-Hill, 1969), IV, p. 437.
5. *Poetry* 30 (April, 1977), 1.
6. Charles J. Seymour in *Masterpieces of Sculpture from The National Gallery of Art* (Washington, D.C., Smithsonian Institute, 1949), p. 14. "It is a figure balanced between awkwardness and grace, between childhood and maturity, between the heroic and the intimate, alert, yet in repose."
7. Pp. 181–185.
8. Janson, *The Sculpture of Donatello*, p. 85.
9. "How, for instance, are we to 'read' the triumphal scene enacted by *putti* on the visor of Goliath's helmet?" Ibid., p. 84.
10. *Atlantic* (November, 1961), p. 172.
11. *The Complete Paintings of Botticelli* (New York, H. N. Abrams, 1967), p. 101.
12. Erwin Panofsky, *Albrecht Dürer* (Princeton, New Jersey, Princeton University Press, 1948), vol. II, p. 152.
13. Dürer's *Death on a Thin Horse*, 1505, possibly inspired by the Nurenburg plague which caused the artist to flee his native city, departs from the "noble rider" concept to feature a crowned skeleton with scythe, clinging to the forelock of an emaciated, belled nag which grins in ugly antithesis to the scowl of Death.
14. (New York, Grossman, 1971), p. 14.
15. As cited in Francis Russell, *The World of Dürer, 1491–1528* (New York, Time, Inc., 1967), p. 123.
16. "One-Way Conversation with Randall Jarrell" in *A Voice from the Hump and a Fourteenth Century Poet's Vision of Christ* (South Brunswick and York, A. B. Barnes, 1977), p. 90.
17. Art-critics Jacques Dupont and François Mathey regard these mysterious diffusions of light as "not just an accessory, but as the subject and almost the purpose of the picture, symbolizing, like the sanctuary lamp, the Divine Presence." *The Seventeenth Century; the New Developments in Art from Caravaggio to Vermeer* (New York, Skira, 1951), p. 36.
18. Possibly after Caravaggio's *Deposition* in the Vatican Museum, sometimes regarded as the source of this canvas, which does indeed recall a Pietà.
19. Jonathan Marshall, "The A. F. A. Convention," *Arts* 31, p. 11.
20. Germaine Bazin, *The History of World Sculpture* (Greenwich, Conn., New York Graphic Society, 1968), p. 136.
21. *A Short History of American Poetry*, p. 372.

22. Yet this Stevens sequence is not one of the fifty–one selections that he singled out for special praise in *The Third Book of Criticism*, pp. 72–73.

23. Bazin, *History of World Sculpture*, p. 300.

24. Jantz (Princeton, N.J., Princeton University Press, 1951), p. 12.

25. Elsewhere (*Shenandoah* 20, 49–87) I have traced other pictorial interests of this writer, who may well have achieved the best translation in English of Goethe's epic, published posthumously after the completion by Lowell of a missing lyric. These, however, concern methodology (as in his imitation of Vuillard strategies) rather than subject.

### Chapter Five

1. November 2, 1967. Inge himself is well qualified to undertake such a study for he was already published, with Vanderbilt's Thomas Young, a book-length examination of worksheets of Donald Davidson, Jarrell's graduate mentor.

2. "Randolph Caldecott: An Appreciation" in *The Randolph Caldecott Treasury*. Selected and edited by Elizabeth L. Billington. (New York and London: Frederick Warne, 1978), p. 12.

3. *The Golden Bird, and Other Fairy Tales of the Brothers Grimm*. New York, Macmillan, 1962.

4. "Rehearsal against Time" in *Poetry* 48, no. 3, June, 1936, 124–25.

5. *Greensboro Daily News*, November 28, 1965. In his Caldecott tribute Sendak writes: " . . . this, of course, is what the illustrator's job is really about—to interpret the text as a musical conductor interprets a score" (p. 13).

6. *Poetry*, December, 1964, p. 105.

7. *Publisher's Weekly*, December 13, 1965, p. 63.

8. *Durham Morning Herald*, October 31, 1965.

9. *The Religion Teacher's Journal*, April, 1978, p. 15.

10. Loneliness as a Jarrell affliction is explored in my *Shenandoah* essay (Winter, 1969, 49–78) listed above; as well as in "Jarrell's Desert of the Heart," *Analects*, Spring, 1961, pp. 24–28.

11. Jarrell prefaces his 1942 parody of Marianne Moore, "The Country Was": "*I hope that it is accurate, admiring, and a little critical.*" The poem is a witty personification of sheep, imitating Miss Moore.

12. In a more pessimistic manner, Rosenthal interprets "The Skaters" and "The Death of the Ball Turret Gunner" as "the symbolic search for the irretrievably lost mother," p. 369.

13. *Durham Morning Herald*, October 31, 1965.

14. *Book Week*, April 17, 1966.

15. *Greensboro Daily News*, November 28, 1965.

16. The young lawyer, L. Richardson Preyer, who shortly after passing the bar took a course from Jarrell, writes in an elegy a year after the death: "He

loved Greensboro, and it was interesting to find references to our town in his work" (*Greensboro Daily News*, October 31, 1965).

17. Letter to author, May 21, 1979.

18. Alan Pryce-Jones "More than Just Child's Play," *Book Week*, October 31, 1965, p. 7.

19. What Sendak attributes to Caldecott in the eulogy cited above is equally true of Jarrell's children's books: "There is no emasculation of truth in his world," p. 14.

20. *Higgelty Piggelty Pop!* (New York, 1967).

21. Cf. 152.

22. As reproduced in *The Biography of a Poem: Jerome* (New York, Grossman, 1971), pp. 58–84. These worksheets hold fascinating revelations, for instance, that "A War," mentioned by at least one critic as his nomination for the best war poem by Jarrell, is included in them, although it was published in a volume earlier than *The Woman at the Washington Zoo*, which contained "Jerome."

### Chapter Six

1. "Plaudits by His Peers for America's Shelley," *New York Herald Tribune*, March 1, 1966. (Written after the Yale memorial the previous evening.)

2. Helen Vendler's approach in reviewing *The Complete Poems* for the *New York Times Book Review*, February 2, 1969, p. 542.

3. "Texts from Housman," Summer, 1935, pp. 260–72.

4. *American Poets from the Puritans to the Present* (Boston, Houghton Mifflin, 1968), p. 370.

5. And earlier, such as in the omnibus review in *Harper's Magazine*, November, 1954, where he asserts that the articles written for the "dead children who read *The Youth's Companion* were usually more thoughtful and demanding, and of more literary merit, than the articles written for the grownups who read the *Post* today." This stricture did not prevent Jarrell from publishing "The Appalling Taste of the Age" (perhaps designedly) in the July 26, 1958, *Post*, 18–19.

6. "The Poet as Humanitarian: Randall Jarrell's Literary Criticism as Self-Revelation," *The South Carolina Review* 10 (November, 1977), 34.

7. This second chapter on Stevens was originally a *Partisan Review*, Spring, 1951, assignment. Janet Sharistanian's Brown University doctoral dissertation had been on determinism in Jarrell.

8. Other essays, fortunately, are in the process of appearing in book form, thanks to Mary Jarrell. Farrar, Straus & Giroux is currently producing *Kipling, Auden & Co.*

9. This essay has been reprinted in *Kipling and the Critics* (New York, 1965), edited with an introduction by Elliot L. Gilbert and numbering among

its contributors T. S. Eliot, C. S. Lewis, Oscar Wilde, Henry James, George Orwell, Lionell Trilling, and Max Beerbohm. Picking the 50 stories the original essay introduced must have been as great sport for Jarrell as teaching them.

10. The widely advertised film version of *The Man Who Would Be King* (1973) televised in June, 1979, was one sign of renewed interest.

11. It is also in the Proceedings of the Festival as published by the Library of Congress, 1964.

12. *Yale Daily News*, April 17, 1964.

13. *Contemporary American Literature 1945–1972*. (New York, Ungar, 1973), p. 116.

14. To offset this reaction, a former Greensboro student, Emily Wilson Herring, writes in a memoir to author dated January 1, 1978: " . . . sometimes I see that the public has enshrined or impaled a different man from the Randall Jarrell we knew. When I read that some poets thought him a cruel critic, I do not recognize him at all. For his students he was the gentlest, kindest, most generous of men."

15. Letter to author April 17, 1978. Wilbur himself has a great sense of humor. Once when asked at the University of Missouri—Kansas City to comment on drugs, he said he couldn't, because he belonged to the "booze age."

16. Ibid.

17. *Southern Review*, Autumn, 1935, one of the uncollected pieces. Subsequently, most of Cather's fans have found this book unsatisfactory.

18. Malkoff, *Crowell's Handbook of American Poetry* (New York, Crowell, 1973), p. 147.

19. (New Brunswick, N.J., Rutgers University Press, 1972), p. 99.

20. Then, a book-length *Jarrell as Critic* should appear. As early as 1954 David Leidig at Vanderbilt did an M.A. thesis on this title.

21. *Newsweek*, December 31, 1956. The caption under his photograph here reads "The Taste of the Age."

22. Flannery O'Connor, on the basis of a chapter in the *Kenyon Review*, felt that *Pictures* was good Jarrell, but not good fiction, lumping it with the novels of Mary McCarthy and her followers. See Sally Fitzgerald (ed.), *The Habit of Being: Letters of Flannery O'Connor* (New York, Farrar, Straus & Giroux, 1979), p. 54.

23. Cited in Curley, Nyren, et al., *Modern American Literature, A Library of Literary Criticism*, II (New York, Ungar, 1969), p. 144.

24. Ibid.

25. "The Sacrosanct Groves of Academe," *New Yorker*, June 19, 1954, p. 93.

26. *The Letters of Wallace Stevens*, selected and edited by Holly Stevens (New York, Alfred A. Knopf, 1977), p. 816.

27. Ibid., p. 875. He felt that *Selected Poems* merited the award.

28. I feel, however, that Sylvia Angus goes too far in her lengthy *Southern*

*Review* analysis of the novel (July 1976), when she says: "It seems likely that this warm, brilliant, and compassionate novel will, more than his poetry, be the work by which Jarrell's creative stature will be judged" (p. 696).

29. The poet knew German well enough to carry on a conversation in that language when abroad, usually when surprised into it.

30. Letter to author, May 15, 1979.

*Chapter Seven*

1. Letter to author, May 21, 1979.

2. Letter to author, January 1, 1978.

3. Robert Humphrey introduced Charles Adams's bibliography: "Jarrell, like Wordsworth, Hopkins, and Frost, ranks among the angels of poetry—those who write for the ear" (p. 12).

4. This might have been the night that Frost's tablecloth was decorated with peacock fantails, recalled over luncheon with me in Norfolk, Virginia, March 3, 1978 by Ann Vernon, roommate of the *Coraddi* editor Ann Duncan and herself a participant in three of Jarrell's courses. Other memories included her teacher's fondness for plaid; the twisted knees under the table, a table which seemed to his regret to separate him from the class.

5. Letter to author April 13, 1978.

6. Letter to author April 13, 1978, with a first paragraph that sounds like a footnote to "A Girl in a Library," Mrs. Miller's apology for delaying to answer my March request: "I, too, teach full-time—a Pfeiffer College assistant professor [in Misenheimer, North Carolina] gets in a terrific tailspin this time of the semester, trying to read all those papers written on the archetypal themes in Beowulf (written by soccer players and drama majors)." She relates how Randall once read at Pfeiffer, where the students adored him, and how he and Mary came later to see Mrs. Miller's newborn Melissa, a missed visit suggesting again "A Girl," with its image of being stood up by the blind date, life. In a second letter (May 21, 1979) she says that although he never saw her two children, he used to send them inscribed books, such as "For Kirk, from Uncle Ramble."

7. "Cinderella" and "The Woman at the Washington Zoo" have also been recorded, with comments, by Jarrell (The Spoken Arts Treasury of 100 American Poets, V, 12). The Madison University of Wisconsin library in its Tape 2134 has Jarrell reading with comments (quite extensive) "Transient Barracks," "Eighth Air Force," "Cinderella," and "The Woman at the Washington Zoo." He concludes these, as he did his classes, with "Thank you very much." *The Poet's Voice*, part of a cassette series originally made at Harvard, includes "The Child of Courts," "A Camp in the Prussian Forest," "Gunner," "The Lines," "A Ward in the States," "Next Day," "Three Bills," and "The Player Piano," also "In Montecito," about which Jarrell jokes with Robert

Lowell, who was in the audience. The 1954 "78" of Jarrell in 1947 reading his own poems at the Library of Congress is almost a collector's item now: L.C., Div. of Music Recording Laboratory, PL 7—"Lady Bates" and "Stalag Luft."

8. Letter to author, May 21, 1979.

9. Among the unexpected titles are the *Everlasting Gospel*, Pushkin's *The Queen of Spades*, Leonov's *Road to the Ocean*, Paul Carroll's *Shadow and Substance*, Samuel Butler's *Notebooks*, Linton's *The Study of Man*, James West's *Plainville, U.S.A.*, Kardiner's *The Individual and Society* and *The Psychological Frontiers of Society*, Malinowski's *The Sexual Life of Savages*, St. Simon's *Memoirs*, Santayana's *The Gospels*. Mann's *Dr. Faustus* (along with R. P. Blackmur's article on it in *Kenyon Review*) is interesting, also the fact that Jarrell cautions Barbara Lovell away from Blake's Prophetic Books, while stressing other Blake items.

10. Letter of May 21, 1979.

11. Letter to author May 15, 1979.

12. Letter to author May 13, 1979. One senses her qualifications, now that as Bertha Harris Wyland she has gone on in professional writing, but the temptation to quote again from one who has seen Shelley plain prompts including this passage: "'You are a poet!' he would announce to one of us; then I and the others would examine our lives, then try to peer into his."

13. Letter to author May 1, 1978. Destined to remain at UNCG Greensboro for his doctorate, Clark has a rare ability to perceive what those who accuse Jarrell of being prosaic miss: "I truly believe poetry must be, if it is any good, music, and I have always tried to write musically."

# Selected Bibliography

PRIMARY SOURCES

1. Collected Works
*The Complete Poems.* New York: Farrar, Straus & Giroux, 1969.
*Poèmes Choisis* présentés et traduits par Renaud de Jouvenal. Paris: P. Seghers, 1965. [Contains English and French versions.]
*Selected Poems.* New York: Atheneum, 1965.

2. Poems
*Blood for a Stranger.* New York: Harcourt, Brace and Co., 1942.
*Little Friend, Little Friend.* New York: Farrar, Straus & Giroux, 1945.
*Losses.* New York: Harcourt, Brace & Co., 1948.
*The Lost World.* New York: Macmillan, 1968.
"The Rage for the Lost Penny," in *Five Young American Poets,* ed. John Ciardi. Norfolk, Conn.: New Directions, 1940, pp. 81–123.
*The Seven-League Crutches.* New York: Harcourt, Brace, Jovanovich, 1957.
*The Woman at the Washington Zoo: Poems and Translations.* New York: Atheneum, 1960.

3. Novel
*Pictures from an Institution.* New York: Knopf, 1954.

4. Criticism
"Implicit Generalization in Housman." Unpublished M.A. thesis, Vanderbilt University, 1939.
*Poetry and the Age.* New York: Vintage Books, 1953.
"Poetry in War and Peace." *Partisan Review,* Winter, 1945, 120–26.
*A Sad Heart at the Supermarket Essays and Fables.* New York: Atheneum, 1962.
*The Third Book of Criticism.* New York: Farrar, Straus & Giroux, 1969.
"Very Graceful Are the Uses of Culture." *Harper's,* November, 1954, pp. 94–105.
*Kipling, Auden & Co./Essays and Reviews 1935–1964.* New York: Farrar, Straus & Giroux, 1980.

5. Editions and Translations

*The Anchor Book of Short Stories. Selected and with an Introduction.* Garden City, New York: Doubleday, 1958.

*The Best Short Stories of Rudyard Kipling.* vii–xix. Garden City, New York: Hanover House, 1961.

*The English in England.* Garden City, New York: Hanover House, 1963.

*Goethe's Faust Part I: An English Translation by Randall Jarrell.* New York: Farrar, Straus & Giroux, 1976.

*The Golden Bird, and Other Fairy Tales of the Brothers Grimm.* Translated and introduced by Randall Jarrell. Illustrated by Sandro Nardini. New York: Macmillan, 1962.

*In the Vernacular: The English in India.* 5–11. Garden City, New York: Doubleday, 1963.

*The Juniper Tree and Other Tales from Grimm,* selected by Lore Segal and Maurice Sendak. New York: Farrar, Straus & Giroux, 1973. Four of the tales translated by Jarrell.

*The Rabbit Catcher and Other Fairy Tales of Ludwig Bechstein.* Translated and introduced by Randall Jarrell. Illustrated by Ugo Fontana. New York: Macmillan, 1962.

*Six Russian Novels.* Introduction by Randall Jarrell, vii–xxxvii. Garden City, New York: Anchor Books, Doubleday, 1963.

*Snow-White and the Seven Dwarfs. A Tale from the Brothers Grimm.* Pictures by Nancy Ekholm Burkert. New York: Farrar, Straus & Giroux, 1972.

*The Three Sisters Anton Chekhov.* Translated by Randall Jarrell, with Afterword. London: Macmillan, 1969.


6. Children's Books

*A Bat Is Born,* from *The Bat-Poet* by Randall Jarrell. Illustrated by John Schoenherr. New York: Doubleday, 1977.

*The Animal Family.* Pictures by Maurice Sendak. New York: Pantheon Books, 1965.

*The Bat-Poet.* Pictures by Maurice Sendak. New York: Macmillan, 1964.

*Fly by Night.* Pictures by Maurice Sendak. New York: Farrar, Straus & Giroux, 1976.

*The Gingerbread Rabbit.* Pictures by Garth Williams. New York: Macmillan, 1964.


7. Miscellaneous

"Answers to Questions," in *Mid-Century American Poets,* ed. John Ciardi. New York: Twayne Publishers, 1950, pp. 182–85.

"The Appalling Taste of the Age." *Saturday Evening Post,* July 26, 1958, pp. 18–19 [with portrait].

SECONDARY SOURCES

1. Bibliographies
ADAMS, CHARLES MARSHALL. *Randall Jarrell, A Bibliography*. Chapel Hill, N.C.: University of North Carolina Press, 1958. Introduction by Robert Humphrey, 11–14. Supplement in *Analects*, I, 49–56.
CALHOUN, RICHARD J. "Towards A Reassessment." *South Atlantic Bulletin* 32 (1967), 1–4. Annotated bibliography.
GILLIKIN, DURE JO. "A Check List of Criticism on Randall Jarrell 1941–1970. With an Introduction and a List of His Major Works." *Bulletin of the New York Public Library* 74 (April, 1971), 176–94. This Greensboro student went on to Chapel Hill for her M.A., choosing as her thesis topic "Conventions in Randall Jarrell's War Poems."
KISSLINGER, MARGARET V. "A Bibliography of Randall Jarrell, 1958–1965." *Bulletin of Bibliography and Magazine Notes* 24 (May–August, 1966), 243–47.
SHAPIRO, KARL. *Randall Jarrell*. Washington, D.C.: Library of Congress, 1967. Description of various kinds of Jarrell materials held by the Library of Congress, including audiovisual.


2. Books and Magazines
*Alumni News*, University of North Carolina at Greensboro, 54 (Spring, 1966). Memorial issue for Jarrell. Students represented and unmentioned above in text include Ineko Kondo, Angela Davis, Pamela Pfaff, and others who graphically re-create "the way it was." Reminiscences also of friends and professional associates.
*Analects* I (Spring, 1964). A short-lived periodical but famous for this issue dedicated to Randall Jarrell, and including tributes by Glauco Cambon, Inigo Seidler, and several more.
CURLEY, DOROTHY NYREN et al. (eds.). *Modern American Literature A Library of Literary Criticism*, II. New York: Frederick Ungar, 1969, 139–44. A good spectrum of critical views.
FERGUSON, SUZANNE. *The Poetry of Randall Jarrell*. Baton Rouge: Louisiana State University Press, 1971. Pioneer study of what after all will remain Jarrell's greatest achievement, the poetry. Photographs included, many obtained from the poet's mother. Thorough scholarship on the work then accessible. She is now compiling a book of essays on Jarrell.
HAGENBÜCHLE, HELEN. *The Black Goddess: A Study of the Archetypal Feminine in the Poetry of Randall Jarrell*. Bern: Francke Verlag, 1975. Though the thesis from which this work originated ignores aspects of Jarrell in substantiating itself, the book generally is of assistance.
HOFFMAN, FREDERICK J. (ed.). *The Achievement of Randall Jarrell: A Comprehensive Selection of His Poems with a Critical Introduction*. Glen-

view, Illinois: Scott, Foresman, 1970. Introduction published separately 1973. While not as brilliant in explication as the University of Wisconsin, Madison, lectures which first awakened my regard for Jarrell, the prefacing remarks in this 86-page volume of the Modern Poets Series are often seminal. At times, however, the comments are negative and capricious.

IVASK, IVAR, and VON WILPERT, GERO. *World Literature Since 1945*. New York: Frederick Ungar, 1973, p. 36. "The Impact of Randall Jarrell (1914–1965) owed something to the very great breadth of his knowledge, his genius in teaching and criticism as well as in poetry."

LOWELL, ROBERT; TAYLOR, PETER; WARREN, ROBERT PENN, (eds.). *Randall Jarrell, 1914–1965*. New York: Farrar, Straus & Giroux, 1967. Marvelous judgment and creativity as to format and decisions relative to space limitations to be credited to Jarrell's old friend, Michael de Capua, publisher's editor. The last essay, "A Group of Two" by Mary Jarrell, pp. 274–99, of tremendous help in "seeing," as he taught others to do. Cleanth Brooks, Denis Donaghue, Karl Shapiro only a few of those eager to offer their "wreaths."

ROSENTHAL, M. L. *Randall Jarrell*. Minneapolis, Minnesota: University of Minnesota Press Pamphlets, 1972. A rather biased handling of Jarrell, reprinted in Denis Donoghue's *Seven American Poets from MacLeish to Nemerov: An Introduction*, as well as in *American Writers: A Collection of Literary Biographies*, II, for which Leonard Unger, once at Greensboro, acted as editor-in-chief. It would seem that a writer as significant as Jarrell should have inspired Mr. Rosenthal to different research.

### 3. Articles and Chapters in Books

ANGUS, SYLVIA. "Randall Jarrell, Novelist: A Reconsideration." *Southern Review* 3 (Summer, 1966), 689–96. Praise of *Pictures*.

ATLAS, JAMES. "Randall Jarrell." *American Poetry Review* 4 (Spring, 1975), 26–28. The strength of Jarrell's colloquial gift praised, and the importance of his political position noted.

BEACH, JOSEPH WARREN. *Obsessive Images*. Minneapolis: University of Minnesota Press, 1960), pp. 178–83. Jarrell's use of the stranger as symbol.

BLOUNT, CHARLOTTE. Winston-Salem *Journal and Sentinel*, July 5, 1966. Discusses resemblance of the bat-poet, hero of the book she is reviewing, to Jarrell himself. Reality of dialogue is singled out for attention.

CALHOUN, RICHARD J. "Randall Jarrell." Cassette Curriculum. Deland, Florida: Everett/Edwards, Inc., 1972. A spoken, 39-minute essay by the editor of the Modern American Poetry Criticism series. Points out: Jarrell anticipated Women's Movement; occasional failure of dream as escape ("The Dead Wingman"); sufferers in the poems as mirrors of our own suffering; the journey as a leading motif; and Jarrell as "a real crowd-pleaser," looking every inch the poet.

CARRUTH, HAYDEN. "Daylight." *Poetry* 105 (December, 1964), 194–95. Review of *The Bat-Poet*. Despite a few kind statements, cruel in a way Jarrell was not: "*The Bat-Poet* is only Remus again: sugar-coated esthetics instead of sugar-coated morality. What a bloody bore!"

——. "Melancholy Monument." *The Nation*, July 7, 1969, pp. 19–21. Review of *The Complete Poems*. High praise of war poems but niggardly as to poetry, criticism, *The Bat-Poet*. Calls Jarrell a Romanticist who, unlike Goethe and Roethke, dwindled away into fragments and exercises.

COX, C. B. "The Painter's Eye." *Spectator*, May 20, 1966. Omnibus Review including *The Lost World*. Prefers "The Lost Children," in which the narrator dreams of early parenthood, the almost-prosaic words not making their own world but referring directly to poignant situations; at worst, sentimental; at best, compassionate and haunting.

DAWSON, SVEN M. "Jarrell's 'The Death of the Ball Turret Gunner.'" *Explicator* 21 (Spring, 1977), Item 29. A few asides on a lyric that (like Yeats and "Innisfree") Jarrell resented as too frequently the only poem that readers connected with him.

DEAGAN, ANN. *There Is No Balm in Birmingham*. Boston: David R. Godine, 1978. Contains "Early November," a poem about visiting Jarrell's grave (pp. 40–42). The author's daughter also has an unpublished poem, "Goodspeed," wherein she describes using Jarrell's plot as a refuge from boys who were throwing sticks at her.

"Desperate Dreams." *Times Literary Supplement*, March 31, 1972, p. 360. Jarrell's childhood as transformed by imagination rather than as a halcyon period, an example of the not uncommon accusation of sentimentality.

DEEN, ROSEMARY [Review of *The Collected Poems*]. *Commonweal*, April 18, 1969, pp. 146–47. Lauds "Nestus Gurley" and asserts that Jarrell ignored T. S. Eliot for Wordsworth.

DONAGHUE, DENIS. "Penny Worlds of the Poets" [Review including *The Lost World*]. *Encounter* 27 (September, 1966), 69–75. His poems are never afraid, ashamed, or proud of their feelings.

DUFFEY, BERNARD. *Poetry in America: Expression and its Values in the Times of Bryant, Whitman, and Pound*. Durham, North Carolina: Duke University Press 1978, pp. 284–87. "For Jarrell, subjective and contemporary experience also meant inclusiveness and contrast." Jarrell's rejection of modernism is a terminal phase of Romantic poetry.

DUNN, DOUGLAS. "An Affable Misery: On Randall Jarrell." *Encounter*, October, 1972, pp. 42–48. This English critic shows a welcome warmth and desire to understand, doubtless owing something of his style to Jarrell's own.

FERGUSON, FRANCES C. "Randall Jarrell and the Flotations of Voice." *Georgia Review* 28 (Fall, 1974), 423–39. An absorbing scrutiny of Jarrellian technique from an unusual angle.

FLINT, R. W. "On Randall Jarrell." *Commentary*, February, 1966, pp. 79–81. A New Critic's retrospective meditation on the poet. Regards war poems as marvelous.

FULLER, JOHN. "Randall Jarrell." In *The Modern Poet*, ed. Ian Hamilton. New York: Horizon Press, 1969, pp. 151–57. Especially insightful re *The Lost World*, and the way that Jarrell uses women in his dramatic monologues.

GRAHAM, W. S. "Jarrell's *Losses:* A Controversy." *Poetry* 72 (September 1948), 302–11. Unbelievably negative estimate, placing Owen, Read, Grenfell, and Rosenberg above Jarrell as war poets. Followed by a refutation by Hayden Carruth.

GRANT, DAMIAN. "Inscape." *The Tablet* 221 (September 10, 1966), 1,019. [Review including *The Lost World*] Quotes Jarrell as to his subject being "*la condition humaine.*" The lost world, Grant sees as that of childhood, evoked throughout with agility. He evaluates book as satisfying and wholly enjoyable, beyond brief praise.

GREENE, GEORGE. "Four Campus Poets." *Thought* 35 (Summer, 1960), 223–47. Review of *The Complete Poems*, one-third on war. Censures excessive notes.

HALL, DONALD. "Nightmares and Irresponsibilities." *New Republic*, December 26, 1960, pp. 18–19. A generally unfavorable estimate.

HASSAN, IHAB. *Contemporary American Literature 1945–1972*. New York: Frederick Ungar, 1973. Somewhat stilted brief account that rises from a liking for Jarrell.

HIDDEN, NORMA. "The Moonlit Door: The Child Image in the Poems of Randall Jarrell." *English* 16 (Summer, 1967), 178–80. Perceptive note on an omnipresent facet of Jarrell imagery.

HILL, H. RUSSELL. "Poetry and Experience." *English Journal* 55 (February, 1966), 162–68. Article written soon after Jarrell's death, which serves to promote classroom study of someone whose appeal to secondary-school students is unique. Good on "A Front," to which Hill devotes six pages based on a tape-recorded California Air-Base seminar.

HIROSE, MICHIJOSHI. "Randall Jarrell and His Agony." In *American Literature in the Forties*. Annual Report, 1975. Tokyo: Tokyo Chapter American Literature Society of Japan, pp. 20–31. An early sign of awareness of Jarrell's worth to Japanese readers, an interest manifested by the "translations in progress" of Fumihisa Matsumoto, who did an M.A. thesis on the poet for Keio University, Tokyo, and now as a member of its staff is enrolled in Yale's American Studies doctoral program.

HUMPHREY, ROBERT. "Randall Jarrell's Poetry." In *Themes and Directions in American Literature*. Lafayette, Indiana: Purdue University, 1969, pp.

220–34. Humphrey's purpose, as in Jarrellian criticism usually, is to identify excellence. Psychoanalytic theory seen as crucial to the lyrics: "Jarrell is as sympathetic as Wordsworth and as outraged as Shelley." Rilke still present as Rilke in Jarrell poetry. Humphrey was a colleague of Jarrell's at the Women's College of the University of North Carolina at Greensboro.

JARRELL, MARY (ed.). "Letters to Vienna." *The American Poetry Review,* July/August, 1977. 11–17. A sampling, with generous commentary weaving them together, of letters from the collection underway. Features the Elizabeth Jarrell came to know during his Salzburg summer, also his letters to Sister Bernetta Quinn.

———. "Peter and Randall." *Shenandoah* 28 (Winter, 1977), 28–34. Peter Taylor memorial issue. A myriad of intimate, funny recollections of an unsurpassed multifriendship.

JOHNSON, CAROL "Randall Jarrell and the Art of Self Defense." *Arts International,* September, 1969, pp. 42–43. Not very responsive to Jarrell's lifelong use of "the remembered child."

KOBLER, JASPER. "Randall Jarrell Seeks Truth in Fantasy." *Forum* [Houston], Spring, 1961, pp. 17–20. A glance at one aspect of Jarrell's epistemology by the author of an M.A. thesis on the poet.

LOGAN, JOHN. "Rilkean Sense." *Saturday Review,* January 28, 1961, pp. 29–30. Review of *The Woman at the Washington Zoo,* which sees Jarrell as, like Rilke, looking within.

MABRY, THOMAS. "'The Tender and the Tough.'" *Sewanee Review* 63 (Winter, 1955), 141–44. Highly readable, though largely negative appraisals of *Pictures.*

MAGUIRE, C. E. "Shape of the Lightning: Randall Jarrell." *Renascence* 7 (Spring, 1955 Summer), 115–20 and 181–86, 195. Believes Gertrude is Jarrell. Maguire a real enthusiast though inclined to underestimate Jarrell's theism. Extremely readable.

MARCUS, MORDECAI and ERIN. "Jarrell's 'The Emancipators.'" *Explicator* 16 (February, 1958), 26. A little light on a seldom-mentioned poem.

MALKOFF, KARL. *Crowell's Handbook of Contemporary American Poetry.* New York: Thomas Y. Crowell Company, 1973, pp. 146–54. A fresher commentary than most of its kind.

MAZZARO, JEROME. "Arnoldian Echoes in the Poetry of Randall Jarrell." *Western Humanities Review* 23 (1969), 314–18. An expected influence, after Jarrell's earnest recommendation to WCUNC freshman Barbara Lovell of *The Scholar Gipsy* and *The Strayed Reveller,* preserved in her list in his handwriting from conferences, of indispensable authors.

———. "Between Two Worlds: The Post-Modernism of Randall Jarrell." *Salmagundi,* Fall, 1971, 93–113. Later appeared in Mazzaro's *Contemporary Poetry in America: Essays and Interviews.* New York: Schocken, 1974, pp. 78–98.

MOON, SAMUEL. "Finding the Lost World." *Poetry* 106 (September, 1965), 425–26. Review of *The Lost World*. Likes the title poem, also "A Hunt in the Black Forest" ("a compelling instance of the child's double values"), but concludes on an unfavorable note.

MORAN, BESS JUNE. *The Seven-League Crutches*. [Review] *The Censer* (College of Saint Teresa, Winona, Minnesota), Spring, 1952, pp. 38–41. Fine explication of "The Black Swan" and "Hohensalzburg." About the latter: "Jarrell's conception of man's nature and destiny is exemplified in this lyric. To him, there is no such thing as permanent death, for in the end one wakes from everything."

NEMEROV, HOWARD. "Randall Jarrell A Myth about Poetry." In *Reflexions on Poetry & Poetics*. New Brunswick, New Jersey: Rutgers University Press, 1972, pp. 96–100. Reviewing *The Complete Poems*, Nemerov balances against the darkness he can't escape in reading them his memory of a congeries of wonderful personality traits in Jarrell. He likens the poet in his use of magic to the sorcerer's apprentice, a comparison recalling Stevens's "Poetry Is a Destructive Force."

NITCHIE, GEORGE W. "Randall Jarrell: A Stand-In's View." *Southern Review* 9 (Autumn, 1973), 883–94. A highly personal encomium in narrative style of the man the writer almost met but never did, whom he yet understands better than most who did meet him, especially in detecting the "unmediated joy" that links Jarrell not only to the often gloomy Rilke but also to the Eliot of *Four Quartets*.

PERRINE, LAWRENCE, and REID, JAMES M., (eds.). *100 American Poems of the Twentieth Century*. New York: 1977, pp. 229–31. Perrine on Greensboro faculty once. Brings out Jarrell's suffering over the tragedy of the Jews, also his explicit use of Saint Paul. "Randall Jarrell sees to it, with bitter eloquence, that we do not forget the monstrous crime of the concentration camp, the mass grave, the death furnace—all these ultimate horrors of the twentieth century." In analyzing "Hope" stresses war's defilement of Christianity.

PREYER, L. RICHARDSON. "A Friend Remembers." *Greensboro Daily News*, October 31, 1965. The recollections of a local lawyer, banker, and tennis player who discovered in Jarrell's modern poetry course the best teacher he was ever to know.

PRYCE-JONES, ALAN. "More than Just Child's Play." *Book Week*, October 31, 1965, p. 5. Review of *The Animal Family*. The title indicates a recognition of serious fiction, as Jarrell himself did in regard to a children's story, telling his cousin Bitsy's daughter: "It really isn't just about *cats*."

QUINN, SISTER M. BERNETTA. "Randall Jarrell: His Metamorphoses." In *The Metamorphic Tradition in Modern Poetry*. New Brunswick: Rutgers University Press, 1955; reprint ed., Staten Island: Gordian Press, 1966, pp. 168–207. Opening paragraph, first written almost thirty years ago, presents Jarrell as perhaps "the most likely candidate among younger writers for a permanent place in American letters." Metamorphosis "is one of Randall Jarrell's ways of voicing that unfathomable disillusion which informs his poetry without ever quite conquering it, because of the child's hope at its heart" (p. 207). A shorter version is in the memorial volume of 1967.

————. "Jarrell's Desert of the Heart." *Analects* I (Spring, 1964), 24–28.

————. "Randall Jarrell: Landscapes of Life and *Life*." *Shenandoah* 20 (Spring, 1969), 49–78. As in *Analects* article, the lyrics are read in terms of symbolic-landscape imagery.

————. "Thematic Imagery in the Poetry of Randall Jarrell." [Review of *The Collected Poems*] *Southern Review* 5 (Autumn, 1969), 126–36. Tracing of dream-star-wish imagery.

————. "Warren and Jarrell: The Remembered Child." *Southern Literary Journal* 8 (Spring, 1976), 24–40. Initiation as a theme in "Time as Hypnosis" and "The Lost World."

RAMSEY, PAUL. "In Exasperation and Gratitude." *Sewanee Review* 74 (Fliot issue, 1976), 930–46. Considers the four-line "A War" (epigram) Jarrell's best war poem. Mostly unfavorable. Accuses Jarrell's personality of intruding. Praise for "The Märchen."

RAY, DAVID. "The Lightning of Randall Jarrell." *Prairie Schooner*, Spring, 1961, pp. 45–52. Representative of the "little magazine" appreciation that Jarrell enjoyed before the coming of a larger audience.

REID, ELIZABETH L. *Richmond Times-Dispatch*, October 4, 1966. Review of *The Bat-Poet*. A characteristic passage: "An unsentimental feeling of goodwill and acceptance, and the author's obvious interest and knowledge of the ways of wild things combine with his skills in the use of good simple prose."

RICHARDS, BERTRAND F. "Jarrell's 'Seele im Raum.'" *Explicator* 33 (November, 1974), Item 22. Some thoughts on a poem which critics increasingly regard as partially autobiographical.

RIDEOUT, WALTER B. "'To Change, to Change!' The Poetry of Randall Jarrell." In *Poets in Progress*, ed. by Edward Hungerford. Evanston, Illinois: Northwestern University Press, 1967, pp. 156–78. An investigation of the import throughout the verse of these "words to live by" that close "The Märchen."

RHYS, BRINLEY. "Chekhov." *Sewanee Review* 78 (1970), 163–76. Covers Daniel Gilles's translation of *The Three Sisters* as well as Jarrell's. Several adverse critical comments. "Jarrell's translation, then, can only be considered as a good auxiliary, but hardly definitive, translation."

ROSS, JAMES. "In Tribute to Randall Jarrell." *Greensboro Daily News*, October 31, 1965. Local persons remember the effect of Jarrell's poetry readings and extol his gift of making people see more deeply into the world.

SAMUELS, CHARLES THOMAS. "Big Pictures and Little Phrases." *The New Republic*, November 29, 1969, pp. 26–30. Extensive review of *The Third Book of Criticism;* negative on Stead but enthusiastic on Auden.

SCANNELL, VERNON. "Not without Glory." In *American Poets of the Second*

*World War.* Beaverton, Oregon: Woburn Press, 1976, pp. 172–237. Although Jarrell wore other hats, it was as a war poet that he first became known; treatment here sensitive and comprehensive.

SHARISTANIAN, JANET. "The Poet as Humanitarian: Randall Jarrell's Literary Criticism as Self-Revelation." *South Carolina Review* 10 (November, 1977), 32–57. Further studies in preparation, hopefully based on this fertile approach of the works as autobiography.

SQUIRES, RADCLIFFE. "The Discrete Poems of Randall Jarrell." *The Southern Review* 9 (Summer, 1973), 745–46. Squires's extensive delvings into Allen Tate's life, intertwined with Randall's, makes any note by him useful.

STAPLES, HUGH B. "Randall Jarrell." *Contemporary Literature* 15 (Summer, 1974), 423–27. Review of Suzanne Ferguson's *The Poetry of Randall Jarrell.* Suggestion that not enough has been done with the worksheets might encourage more studies like Mary Jarrell's on "Jerome." Praise for analysis of the neglected "Donatello" lyric.

STEPANCHEV, STEPHEN. "Randall Jarrell." In *American Poetry since 1945.* New York: Harper & Row, 1965, pp. 37–52. Rather pedestrian but not to be ignored because of the paucity of overall treatments.

TAYLOR, PETER. "That Cloistered Jazz." *Michigan Quarterly Review* 5 (Fall, 1966), 237–45. Valuable because of the mutual devotion and understanding that existed between Taylor and Jarrell, from the years at Vanderbilt onward.

TYLER, PARKER. "The Dramatic Lyricism of Randall Jarrell." *Poetry* 79 (March, 1952), 335–46. Two sides of the poet singled out for praise at what was almost the outset of his career. A brilliantly original review of *The Seven-League Crutches.*

WATSON, ROBERT. "A Colleague's View." *Greensboro Daily News,* October 31, 1965. Watson, who was teaching with Jarrell the semester of the latter's death, praises *The Lost World* in particular; their friendship lends his "view" cogency.

WEISBERG, ROBERT. "Randall Jarrell: The Integrity of His Poetry." *Centennial Review* 17 (Summer, 1973), 237–56. One of the best coverages, stressing his belief that the poems are epiphanies.

WILCOTT, PAUL. "Randall Jarrell's Eschatological Vision." *Renascence* 18 (Summer, 1966), 210–15. Misleading title, since it centers on Lowell's "Over the Rainbow," although it does involve Jarrell's comments on Lowell in *Poetry and the Age.*

# Index